EXPLORING CONIC SECTIONS

with

THE GEOMETER'S SKETCHPAD®

DANIEL SCHER

Key Curriculum Press
Innovators in Mathematics Education

Exploring Conic Sections with *The Geometer's Sketchpad*

Project Editor:	Steven Chanan
Production Editor:	Jennifer Strada
Art and Design Coordinator:	Caroline Ayres
Art Editor:	Jason Luz
Copyeditor:	Joan Saunders
Manager, Editorial Production:	Debbie Cogan
Production Director:	Diana Jean Parks
Cover Designer:	Ariana Grabec–Dingman
Cover Photo Credits:	© Private Collection, Bridgeman Art Library; © Paul Eekhof, Masterfile
Prepress and Printer:	Data Reproductions
Executive Editor:	Casey FitzSimons
Publisher:	Steven Rasmussen

Cover art and text include illustrations from *Sive de Organica Conicarum Sectionum in Plano Descriptione, Tractatus* by Frans van Schooten (Leiden, 1646). An original copy of this book is housed at Cornell's Kroch Library.

Limited Reproduction Permission

Exploring Conic Sections Sketches Disk

Key Curriculum Press guarantees that the Sketches Disk that accompanies this book is free of defects in materials and workmanship. A defective disk will be replaced free of charge if returned within 90 days of the purchase date. After 90 days, there is a $10.00 replacement fee.

Key Curriculum Press
1150 65th Street
Emeryville, California 94608
510-595-7000
editorial@keypress.com
http://www.keypress.com

10 9 8 7 6 5 4 3 2 1   05 04 03 02 01   ISBN 1-55953-533-4

Contents

Introduction

First, a confession: As a student, I didn't place conic sections on my list of favorite high-school topics.

The standard textbook treatment of the ellipse, parabola, and hyperbola seemed uninspired. There were messy algebraic equations with multiple square roots. There was lots of terminology. Drawing a conic meant plotting several points on graph paper and connecting them with a wobbly curve.

I gave little thought to conics until I met David Dennis, then a fellow graduate student in mathematics education at Cornell University.

David had a keen interest in the origins of curve-drawing devices. One historical figure in particular intrigued him: Frans van Schooten (1615–1660), a Dutch mathematician whose translation and commentary for Descartes' landmark treatise, *La Géométrie*, led to the popularization of Cartesian geometry.

Descartes' book was available in bookstores, but van Schooten's work, *Sive de Organica Conicarum Sectionum in Plano Descriptione, Tractatus* (*A Treatise on Devices for Drawing Conic Sections*), remained tucked away in rare book collections. Luckily, Cornell's Kroch Library contained a copy. David made the trip.

When he returned from the library, David could barely contain his enthusiasm. "Go and see it for yourself," he said. "It's really something."

A visit to the library confirmed David's findings. There in van Schooten's book were drawing after drawing of devices that drew conics. The illustrations were exquisite, with artistic flourishes adorning many of them.

Viewing van Schooten's curve-drawing devices dispelled any notions that mathematical manipulatives were a modern invention. Van Schooten had beaten us all to the punch more than 350 years ago.

An illustration from the title page of van Schooten's book

As I paged through van Schooten's book, I wondered whether his ideas could find their way into today's mathematics classrooms. His models, consisting of hinges and slotted rulers, were not always simple to build. How could students replicate them?

Sketchpad provided a large part of the answer.

While nothing can substitute for the experience of operating a physical model, a Sketchpad simulation comes close. In fact, Sketchpad betters van Schooten in some ways, allowing students to manipulate the parameters of any model and view their effects on a curve immediately.

Not every activity in this book originates from a van Schooten device, but all share the belief that the method for producing a curve is as important as the curve itself.

Customizing the Activities

The activities in this collection are designed with flexible learning options in mind. Each chapter opens with an overview of the various pathways you might follow through the material.

If constructing physical devices isn't your interest, then skip to the corresponding Sketchpad models. These can be built from scratch or opened pre-made on the accompanying CD-ROM. If you'd like to understand why the various curve-drawing devices work, you can follow along with hints or strike out on your own to create an original proof. You can complete the entire section of ellipse activities or choose a set of interrelated activities spanning all three conics.

Any of these choices could be a sensible option for your needs.

Conic sections form the centerpiece of this book but are not the only mathematics under study. Issues of congruency, similarity, the Pythagorean theorem, trigonometry, and geometric optimization all arise naturally while studying the ellipse, parabola, and hyperbola.

This book represents a marriage of 17th-century manipulatives with 21st-century technology. Enjoy the partnership.

Acknowledgments

As the preceding introduction makes clear, this book would not exist without David Dennis. His enthusiasm and knowledge of the field contributed immeasurably to this book's content.

Al Cuoco and E. Paul Goldenberg from Education Development Center, Inc. had the clever idea to use ellipses to solve optimization problems geometrically. The optimization material in this book draws from their chapter, "Dynamic Geometry as a Bridge from Euclidean Geometry to Analysis," in *Geometry Turned On* (Mathematical Association of America, 1997).

Nick Jackiw suggested several of the sketches in this book. He also built the nifty parabola-drawing device shown on the back cover.

Bill Finzer served as my editor for the first edition of this book. His expert guidance laid the groundwork for this revised and expanded edition. As my new editor, Steven Chanan found ways to push the conics material in new directions. It's a much better book for his efforts.

Despina Stylianou and Beth Porter provided valuable feedback on the initial draft of these materials.

Finally, I thank my New York University graduate students for their help in testing these activities.

Common Commands and Shortcuts

Below are some common Sketchpad actions used throughout this book. In time, these operations will become familiar, but at first you may want to keep this list by your side.

To create a new sketch

Choose **New Sketch** from the File menu.

To close a sketch

Choose **Close** from the File menu. Or click in the close box in the upper-left (Mac) or upper-right (Windows) corner of the sketch.

To undo or redo a recent action

Choose **Undo** from the Edit menu. You can undo as many steps as you want, all the way back to the state your sketch was in when last opened. To redo, choose **Redo** from the Edit menu.

To deselect everything

Click in any blank area of your sketch with the **Arrow** tool or press Esc until objects deselect. Do this before making selections required for a command so that no extra objects are included. To deselect a single object while keeping all other objects selected, click on it with the **Arrow** tool.

To show or hide a label

Position the finger of the **Text** tool over the *object* and click. The hand will turn black when it's correctly positioned to show or hide a label.

To change a label

Position the finger of the **Text** tool over the *label* and double-click. The letter "A" will appear in the hand when it's correctly positioned.

To change an object's line width or color

Select the object and choose from the appropriate submenu in the Display menu.

To hide an object

Select the object and choose **Hide** from the Display menu.

To construct a segment's midpoint

Select the segment and choose **Midpoint** from the Construct menu.

To construct a parallel line

Select a straight object for the new line to be parallel to and a point for it to pass through. Then choose **Parallel Line** from the Construct menu.

To construct a perpendicular line

Select a straight object for the new line to be perpendicular to and a point for it to pass through. Then choose **Perpendicular Line** from the Construct menu.

To reflect a point (or other object)

Double-click the mirror (any straight object) or select it and choose **Mark Mirror**. Then select the point (or other object) and choose **Reflect** from the Transform menu.

To trace an object

Select the object and choose **Trace** from the Display menu. Do the same thing to toggle tracing off. (If you'd rather that traces not fade, uncheck Fade Traces Over Time on the Preferences Color panel.)

To use the calculator

Choose **Calculate** from the Measure menu. To enter a measurement into a calculation, click on the measurement itself in the sketch.

Keyboard shortcuts

Command	Mac	Windows
Undo	⌘+Z	Ctrl+Z
Redo	⌘+R	Ctrl+R
Select All	⌘+A	Ctrl+A
Properties	⌘+?	Alt+?
Hide Objects	⌘+H	Ctrl+H
Show/Hide Labels	⌘+K	Ctrl+K
Trace Objects	⌘+T	Ctrl+T
Erase Traces	⌘+B	Ctrl+B

Command	Mac	Windows
Animate/Pause	⌘+`	Alt+`
Increase Speed	⌘+]	Alt+]
Decrease Speed	⌘+[	Alt+[
Midpoint	⌘+M	Ctrl+M
Intersection	⌘+I	Ctrl+I
Segment	⌘+L	Ctrl+L
Polygon Interior	⌘+P	Ctrl+P
Calculate	⌘+=	Alt+=

Action	Mac	Windows
scroll drag	Option+ drag	Alt+drag
display Context menu	Control+ click	right-click
navigate Toolbox	Shift+arrow keys	
choose **Arrow**, deselect objects, stop animations, erase traces	Esc (escape key)	
move selected objects 1 pixel	←, ↑, →, ↓ keys (hold down to move continuously)	

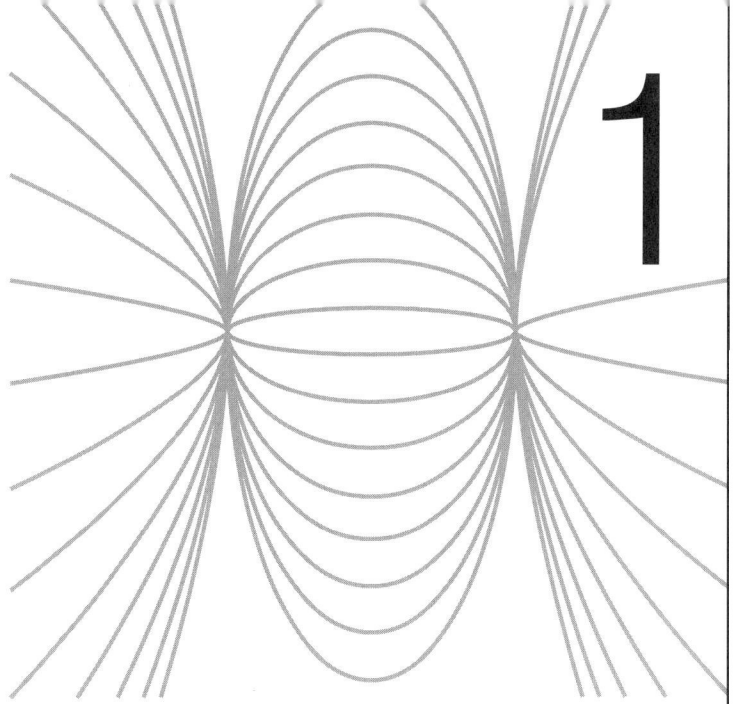

Ellipses

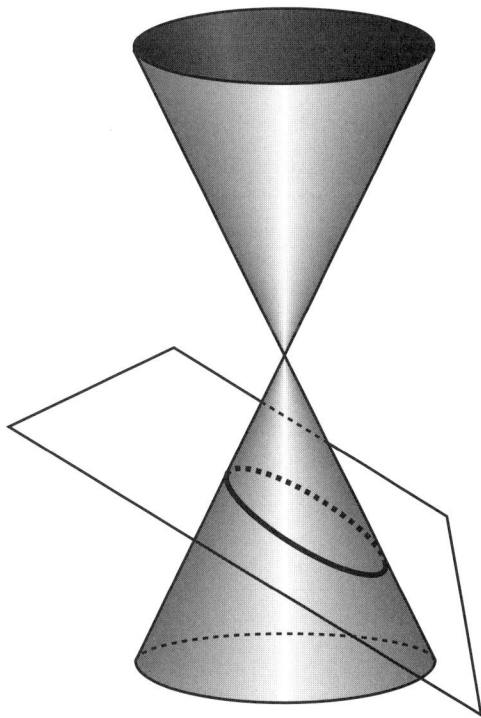

CHAPTER OVERVIEW

Of all the conic sections, the ellipse is the one we see most often. Any circle, when viewed at an angle, appears elliptical. Tilt a drinking glass and the water along the surface outlines an ellipse. Place a ball on the floor and shine an angled beam of light onto it from above—the ball will cast an elliptical shadow on the floor. Slice a cone at an angle from side to side (as shown at right) and the cross section is an ellipse. (This explains why the ellipse qualifies as a conic section.) On a grander scale, the orbits of planets trace ellipses. Comets in permanent orbit around the sun follow elliptical paths.

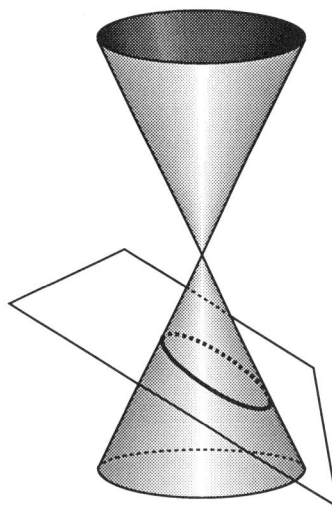

When a plane cuts only one of two cones forming a double-cone, the result is a circle or an ellipse. If the cut is perpendicular to the double-cone's axis, the result is a circle; otherwise, it's an ellipse.

The material in this chapter falls into three general categories:

- Activities I–IV introduce basic ellipse terminology (focal points, major/minor axes, eccentricity) and common ellipse construction techniques (on paper and with Sketchpad).

- Activities V and VI offer two lesser-known constructions that call upon the ellipse's distance definition for their proofs.

- The constructions in activities VII and VIII highlight algebraic proofs.

In total, this chapter offers thirteen ellipse constructions for you to sample. Open the multi-page sketch **Ellipse Tour.gsp** for a handy slide-show overview.

I. Getting Started: When Is a Circle Not a Circle?

Introduce yourself to ellipses as a Sketchpad circle splits its center into two. Start your ellipse explorations here.

II. The Pins-and-String Construction

Swing a string (literally!) to draw an ellipse. Then use a Sketchpad model to formulate an ellipse's distance definition.

III. The Concentric Circles Construction

Two sets of concentric circles set the stage for this classic Sketchpad ellipse construction.

IV. Some Ellipse Relationships

Investigate a pre-built Sketchpad model to uncover the algebraic and geometric relationships between an ellipse's major axis, minor axis, focal length, and eccentricity.

V. The Folded Circle Construction

Watch an ellipse appear before your eyes as you fold and unfold a paper circle. Model the technique with Sketchpad to reveal the underlying mathematics.

VI. The Congruent Triangles Construction

A pair of congruent triangles holds the key to this unusual Sketchpad ellipse construction.

VII. The Carpenter's Construction

Roll up your sleeves as you build a carpenter's ellipsograph with a ruler and then with Sketchpad.

VIII. Danny's Ellipse

High school student Danny Vizcaino knew there had to be a better way to construct a Sketchpad ellipse. He was right. Read all about it!

IX. Ellipse Projects

Round out the chapter with some enticing ellipse excursions.

Getting Started: When Is a Circle Not a Circle?

Below is a circle with center at point C.

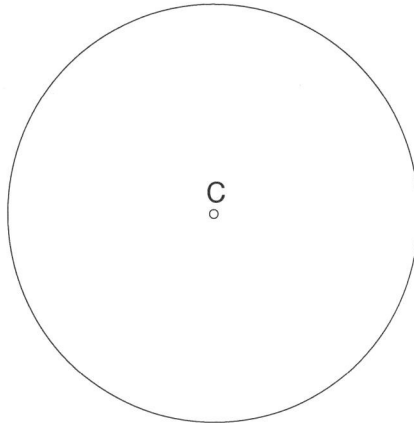

Imagine that the circle's center splits into two points, F_1 and F_2. As the points move away from each other, the circle deforms to accommodate these two "centers." The circle is now an ellipse.

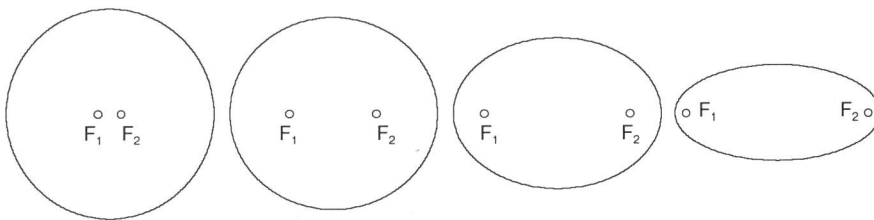

F_1 and F_2 have special names. They're called the **focal points** or **foci** (singular: **focus**) of the ellipse.

Open the sketch **Stretch.gsp** in the **Ellipse** folder. You'll see a circle . . . or is it? Drag the circle's center and watch what happens.

We draw circles by using a compass. But how can we draw ellipses? The pins-and-string activity that follows offers one possibility.

The Pins-and-String Construction   Name(s): _____

There are many ways to construct an ellipse, but perhaps the most well-known method involves just two thumbtacks and a length of string. You'll use these materials now to build ellipses by hand. In the next activity, you'll model a similar technique with Sketchpad.

Constructing a Physical Model

Preparation: You'll need a piece of string, two thumbtacks, a corkboard, a large sheet of paper, and a pencil.

1. Place your paper on top of the corkboard and stick the two thumbtacks into it. Then tie each end of the string onto a thumbtack.

   Pick any locations for the thumbtacks, but make sure to leave some slack in the string. The thumbtacks will be the focal points of your ellipse.

From *Sive de Organica Conicarur Sectionum in Plano Descriptione, Tractatus*, by Dutch mathematicia Frans van Schooten, 1646.

2. Pull the string taut with your pencil. Make sure the string lies near the tip of the pencil.

3. Keeping the string taut, swing the pencil around the focal points, letting the tip of the pencil trace its path. You may need to reposition the pencil to draw the entire curve.

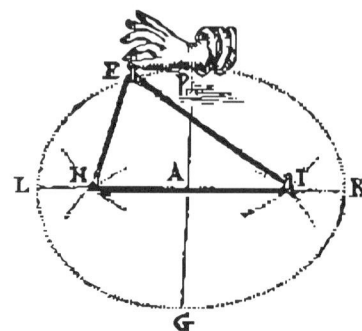

Questions

Q1 What symmetries do you see in your ellipse? Draw a picture to illustrate any lines of symmetry.

Q2 Move the ends of your string so that they're farther apart. Redraw the ellipse and describe how its shape compares to your original curve.

Q3 Move the ends of your string close together. Redraw the ellipse and describe how its shape compares to your original curve.

Q4 Suppose you move the ends of your string so far apart that the string is fully extended and taut. What "curve" will your pencil draw?

Q5 Suppose you attach both ends of the string to the same thumbtack. What curve will your pencil draw?

Q6 Suppose a friend wants to draw an ellipse identical to one of yours. What two pieces of information would you need to give her so that she could reproduce it?

Q7 There are two important segments associated with every ellipse: the *major axis* and the *minor axis*. In each of the following illustrations, segment AB is the major axis, segment CD is the minor axis, and F_1 and F_2 are the focal points.

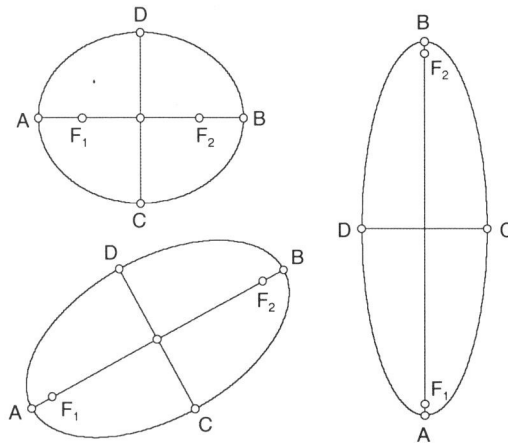

Based on these pictures, write your own definition of the major and minor axes.

Q8 Without using any tools, how could you form the major and minor axes of an ellipse cut out of paper?

Uncover the Imposter

Open the sketch **Points.gsp** in the **Ellipse** folder. You'll see two foci, F_1 and F_2, of an invisible ellipse and three points, A, B, and C. The ellipse passes through exactly two of these three points, but which ones?

Use Sketchpad's measurement and calculation tools to spot the imposter.

Q9 Which point doesn't sit on the ellipse? Explain how you can tell.

Q10 Complete this sentence without mentioning of pins or string:

An ellipse is the set of points P such that the following value is constant for all locations of P: _____

Explore More

1. Open the sketch **Parametric Ellipses.gsp** (**Ellipse** folder) to view ellipses constructed with Sketchpad's parametric coloring feature.

2. Here is the definition of a new curve similar to an ellipse:

The set of points P such that $PA + PB + PC$ is constant for three fixed points, A, B, and C.

Open the sketch **New Curve.gsp** (**Ellipse** folder) to see how such a curve can be constructed using Sketchpad's parametric coloring feature.

The Concentric Circles Construction   Name(s): _____

Circles that are concentric share the same center. In this activity, you'll use two sets of concentric circles to draw an ellipse by hand. You'll then transfer this technique to Sketchpad to draw an ellipse whose shape and size can be adjusted just by dragging your mouse.

Sketching Ellipses by Hand

The illustration below shows two sets of concentric circles. One set of circles is centered at point F_1, the other at point F_2. For each set, the radii of the circles increase by 1's, from 1 unit all the way up to 6 units.

Points F_1 and F_2 are the foci of an infinite number of ellipses, but only two that we're interested in: the one that passes through point A and the one that passes through point B.

Q1 How many units apart are points A and F_1? How many units apart are points A and F_2? What is the numerical value of $AF_1 + AF_2$?

Remember: An ellipse is the set of points P such that $PF_1 + PF_2$ is constant.

Q2 Locate and mark at least seven points that sit on the ellipse passing through point A. Explain how you found them.

Q3 Locate and mark at least seven other points that sit on the ellipse passing through point B. (Use a different colored pen or pencil if possible.) Explain how you found them.

Q4 Using the points you found as guidelines, sketch the two ellipses.

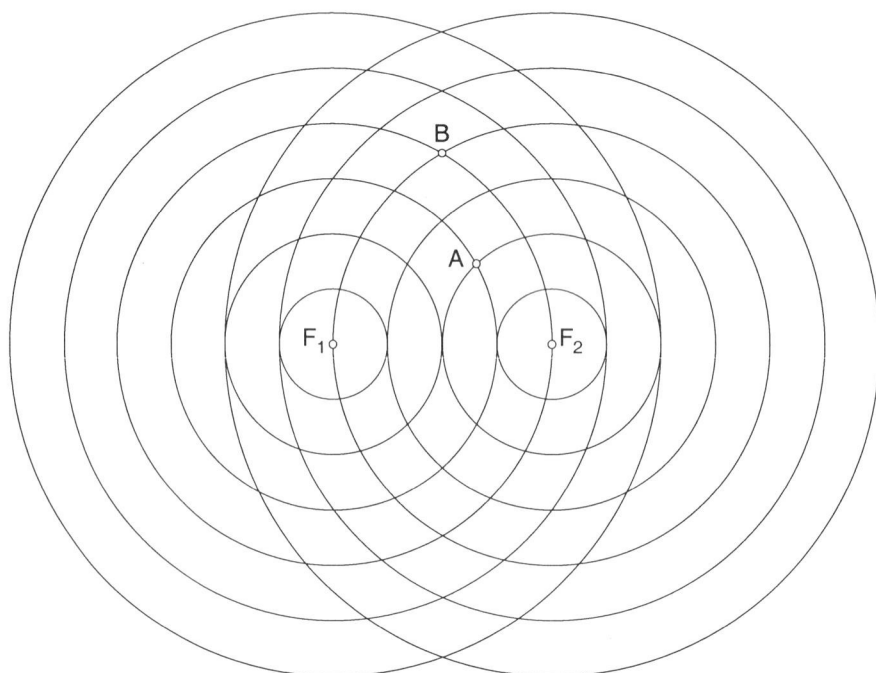

Constructing a Sketchpad Model

Now that you've drawn some ellipses by hand, it's time to build a dynamic one: an ellipse that changes shape as its parts are dragged. Follow the steps below to construct a Sketchpad ellipse. As you do, think about how this method relates to the concentric circles technique.

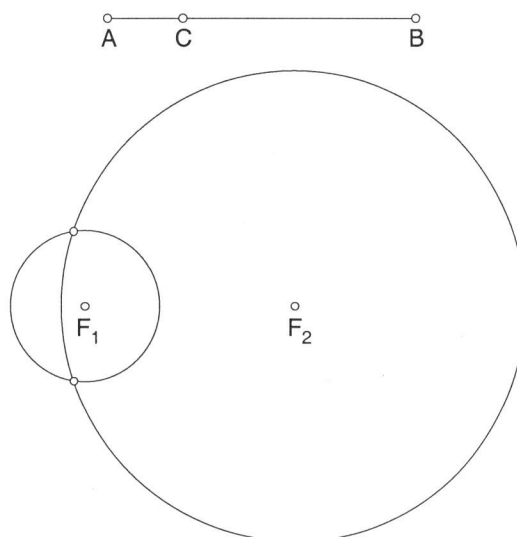

1. Draw a horizontal line near the top of your screen. Hide the control points by selecting them and choosing **Hide Points** from the Display menu.

2. Construct points A, B, and C on the line. The location of these points doesn't matter, but make sure point C is between points A and B.

3. Hide the line. Draw individual segments AC and CB.

4. Draw points F_1 and F_2 to represent the foci of your ellipse.

5. Using the **Circle by Center+Radius** command, construct a circle with center F_1 and radius AC. Construct another circle with center F_2 and radius CB.

6. Construct the intersection points of the circles. (You might have to adjust your model so the circles intersect.)

7. Select the intersection points and choose **Trace Intersections** from the Display menu.

If you don't want your traces to fade, be sure the Fade Traces Over Time box is unchecked on the Color panel of the Preferences dialog box.

8. Drag point C back and forth slowly along $\overline{AB}$ and observe the trace of the two points.

9. Change the distance between F_1 and F_2. Then, if necessary, choose **Erase Traces** from the Display menu to erase your previous curve. Trace several new curves, each time varying the distance between the focal points.

The Concentric Circles Construction (continued)

For every new location of F_1 and F_2, you need to retrace your curve. Ideally, your ellipse should adjust automatically as you drag either focus. Sketchpad's powerful **Locus** command makes this possible.

10. Turn tracing off for the two intersection points by selecting them and once again choosing **Trace Intersections** from the Display menu.

11. Select one of the two intersection points and point C. Choose **Locus** from the Construct menu. Do this again for the other intersection point and point C. You'll form an entire curve: the locus of the two intersection points as point C moves along segment AB.

    Drag F_1, F_2, or point B to change the size and shape of the ellipse.

Questions

Q5 As you drag point C along segment AB, the radii of both circles change lengths. Still, there is a relationship that exists between the two radii regardless of point C's position. What is it?

Q6 Explain why the two intersection points of the two circles trace an ellipse.

Q7 How far apart can the two focal points be before you can no longer trace an ellipse?

Q8 Select your two onscreen circles, choose **Trace Circles** from the Display menu, then drag point C along segment AB.

Based on this experiment, describe the similarities between your Sketchpad construction and the concentric circles technique.

Explore More

1. By shortening the distance between points A and B and dragging point C to the left of A and to the right of B so that it does not lie between them, it's possible to draw a different type of curve. Try it and see what you get.

2. Consider the definition of a *constant-perimeter rectangle*:

   > A *constant-perimeter rectangle* is a rectangle constructed in Sketchpad whose dimensions can change, but whose perimeter always remains fixed at a given, constant value.

   This means that a rectangle with constant perimeter of 20 inches could have dimensions of $3'' \times 7''$, $6'' \times 4''$, or $2'' \times 8''$, but *not* $5'' \times 6''$.

   Use the techniques you learned when building a Sketchpad ellipse to construct a constant-perimeter rectangle.

Some Ellipse Relationships

Name(s): _____

In the Pins-and-String activity, you drew ellipses with a pencil and a taut piece of string. Now, you'll use Sketchpad to explore some of the algebraic and geometric relationships that exist between this string and an ellipse's major and minor axes.

Finding Lengths

Open the sketch **String.gsp** in the **Ellipse** folder. You'll see an ellipse with major axis AB, minor axis CD, and focal points at F_1 and F_2.

Point P represents the pencil point that's pulling taut a string attached to points F_1 and F_2. Together, segments PF_1 and PF_2 represent the string.

The total length of the "string" is 20 cm ($PF_1 + PF_2$). The distance between F_1 and F_2 is 16 cm.

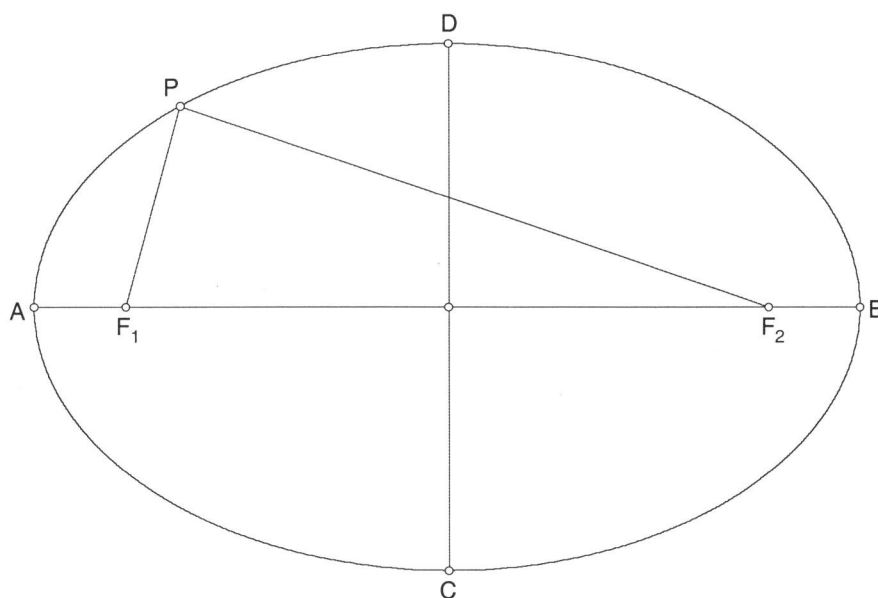

Questions

Answer these questions *without* taking any measurements with Sketchpad. For each one, drag point P around the ellipse until you find a location that helps you answer the question.

Q1 What is the length of the major axis AB? Explain where you positioned point P to reach your conclusion.

Q2 What is the length of the minor axis CD? Explain where you positioned point P to reach your conclusion.

Some Ellipse Relationships (continued)

Eccentricity

Some ellipses are "skinny" and elongated. Others are "fat" and nearly circular. The eccentricity of an ellipse is a measure that captures the shape of an ellipse in one numerical value.

> The **eccentricity** of an ellipse is defined as:
>
> $$\frac{\text{the distance between the focal points}}{\text{the distance between the endpoints of the major axis}}$$

1. Open the sketch **Eccentricity.gsp** in the **Ellipse** folder. You'll see an ellipse with major axis endpoints A and B, and focal points F_1 and F_2.

2. Use Sketchpad's **Distance** command to measure the two distances needed to compute the ellipse's eccentricity.

3. Use Sketchpad's **Calculate** command to compute the eccentricity.

Questions

Q3 Your Sketchpad ellipse can change its size and shape to represent a whole collection of ellipses. Before experimenting with it, make a prediction: How small and how large do you think an ellipse's eccentricity can become? Explain your reasoning.

Q4 Use points B and D of your sketch to change the size and shape of the ellipse. As you do so, monitor the values of its eccentricity. Does your prediction from Q3 hold? Modify it if necessary.

Q5 How many ellipses can share the same eccentricity? How could you create two ellipses with the same eccentricity without using Sketchpad?

Explore More

See Q2 from earlier in the activity for help with this construction. →

1. Open the second page of the sketch **String.gsp.** You'll see a new ellipse along with the length of "string" used to draw it. Construct the focal points of the ellipse. No measuring allowed!

   Make sure your foci are *dynamic:* they should adjust themselves to remain in the proper locations as you change the length of the string.

2. Johannes Kepler's First Law of planetary motion states that the orbit of each planet is an ellipse with the Sun at one focus. Do some research to find the eccentricities of our planets. Why might astronomers before Kepler have believed planets moved in circular motion?

The Folded Circle Construction   Name(s): _____

Sometimes a conic section appears in the unlikeliest of places. In this activity, you'll explore a paper-folding construction in which crease lines interact in a surprising way to form a conic.

Constructing a Physical Model

Preparation: Use a compass to draw a circle with a radius of approximately three inches on a piece of wax paper or patty paper. Cut out the circle with a pair of scissors. (If you don't have these materials, you can draw the circle in Sketchpad and print it.)

1. Mark point A, the center of your circle.

2. Mark a random point B within the interior of your circle.

> If you're working in a class, have members place B at different distances from the center. If you're working alone, do this section twice—once with B close to the center, once with B close to the edge.

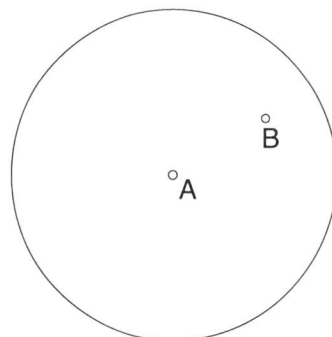

3. As shown below right, fold the circle so that a point on its circumference lands directly onto point B. Make a sharp crease to keep a record of this fold. Unfold the circle.

4. Fold the circle along a new crease so that a different point on the circumference lands on point B. Unfold the circle and repeat the process.

5. After you've made a dozen or so creases, examine them to see if you spot any emerging patterns.

> Mathematicians would describe your set of creases as an **envelope** of creases.

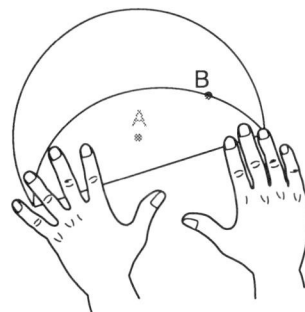

6. Resume creasing your circle. Gradually, a well-outlined curve will appear. Be patient—it may take a little while.

7. Discuss what you see with your classmates and compare their folded curves to yours. If you're doing this activity alone, fold a second circle with point B in a different location.

Questions

Q1 The creases on your circle seem to form the outline of an ellipse. What appear to be its focal points?

Q2 If you were to move point *B* closer to the edge of the circle and fold another curve, how do you think its shape would compare to the first curve?

Q3 If you were to move point *B* closer to the center of the circle and fold another curve, how do you think its shape would compare to the first curve?

Constructing a Sketchpad Model

Fold and unfold. Fold and unfold. Creasing your circle takes some work. Folding one or two sheets is fun, but what would happen if you wanted to continue testing different locations for point *B*? You'd need to keep starting with fresh circles, folding new sets of creases.

Sketchpad can streamline your work. With just one circle and one set of creases, you can drag point *B* to new locations and watch the crease lines adjust themselves instantaneously.

8. Open a new sketch and use the **Compass** tool to draw a large circle with center *A*. Hide the circle's radius point.

9. Use the **Point** tool to draw a point *B* at a random spot inside the circle.

10. Construct a point *C* on the circle's circumference.

11. Construct the "crease" formed when point *C* is folded onto point *B*.

12. Drag point *C* around the circle. If you constructed your crease line correctly, it should adjust to the new locations of point *C*.

13. Select the crease line and choose **Trace Line** from the Display menu.

> If you don't want your traces to fade, be sure the Fade Traces Over Time box is unchecked on the Color panel of the Preferences dialog box.

14. Drag point *C* around the circle to create a collection of crease lines.

15. Drag point *B* to a different location and then, if necessary, choose **Erase Traces** from the Display menu.

16. Drag point *C* around the circle to create another collection of crease lines.

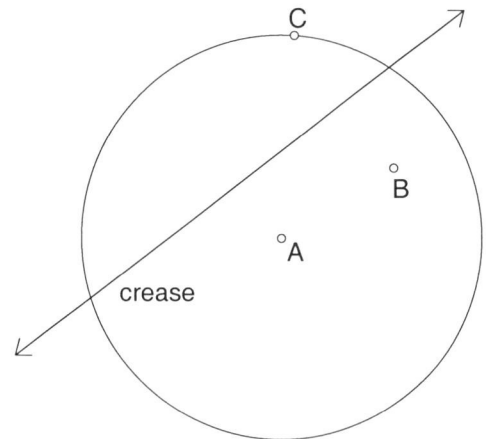

The Folded Circle Construction (continued)

Retracing creases for each location of point *B* is certainly faster than folding new circles. But we can do better. Ideally, your crease lines should relocate automatically as you drag point *B*. Sketchpad's powerful **Locus** command makes this possible.

17. Turn tracing off for your original crease line by selecting it and once again choosing **Trace Line** from the Display menu.

18. Now select your crease line and point *C*. Choose **Locus** from the Construct menu. An entire set of creases will appear: the locus of crease locations as point *C* moves along its path. If you drag point *B*, you'll see that the crease lines readjust automatically.

19. Save your sketch as **Creased Circle.gsp**. You'll use it again in one of the Hyperbola Projects activities.

Questions

Q4 How does the shape of the curve change as you move point *B* closer to the edge of the circle?

Q5 How does the shape of the curve change as you move point *B* closer to the center of the circle?

The **Merge** and **Split** commands appear in the Edit menu. → **Q6** Select point *B* and the circle. Then merge point *B* onto the circle's circumference. Describe the crease pattern.

Q7 Select point *B* and split it from the circle's circumference. Then merge it with the circle's center. Describe the crease pattern.

Playing Detective

Each crease line on your circle touches the ellipse at exactly one point. Another way of saying this is that each crease is *tangent* to the ellipse. By engaging in some detective work, you can locate these tangency points and use them to construct just the ellipse without its creases.

20. Open the sketch **Folded Circle.gsp** in the **Ellipse** folder. You'll see a thick crease line and its locus already in place.

21. Drag point *C* and notice that the crease line remains tangent to the ellipse. The exact point of tangency lies at the intersection of two lines—the crease line and another line not shown here. Construct this line in your sketch as well as the point of tangency, point *E*.

Select the locus and make its width thicker so that it's easier to see. → 22. Select point *E* and point *C* and choose **Locus** from the Construct menu. If you've identified the tangency point correctly, you should see a curve appear precisely in the white space bordered by the creases.

The Folded Circle Construction (continued)

How to Prove It

The Folded Circle construction seems to generate ellipses. Can you prove that it does? Try developing a proof on your own, or work through the following steps and questions.

The picture at right should resemble your construction. Line *HI* (the perpendicular bisector of segment *CB*) represents the crease formed when point *C* is folded onto point *B*. Point *E* sits on the curve itself.

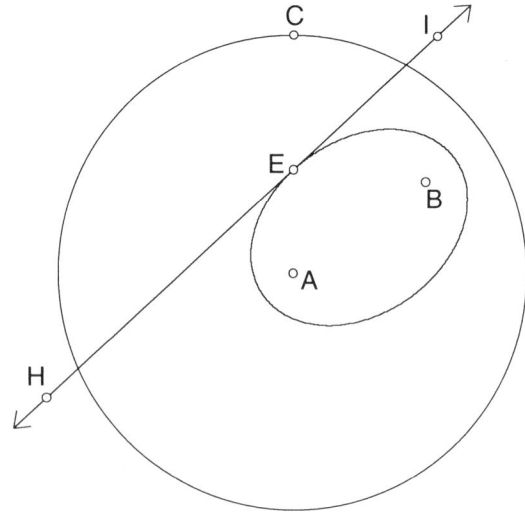

23. Add segments *CB*, *BE*, and *AC* to the picture.

24. Label the intersection of $\overline{CB}$ with the crease line as point *D*.

Questions

Q8 Use a triangle congruence theorem to prove that $\triangle BED \cong \triangle CED$.

Q9 Segment *BE* is equal in length to which other segment? Why?

Remember: An ellipse is the set of points such that the sum of the distances from each point to two fixed points (the foci) is constant.

Q10 Use the distance definition of an ellipse and the result from Q9 to prove that point *E* traces an ellipse.

Explore More

1. When point *B* lies within its circle, the creases outline an ellipse. What happens when point *B* lies *outside* its circle?

2. Use the illustration from your ellipse proof to show that $\angle AEH = \angle BED$.

   Here's an interesting consequence of this result: Imagine a pool table in the shape of an ellipse with a hole at one of its focal points. If you place a ball on the other focal point and hit it in *any* direction without spin, the ball will bounce off the side and go straight into the hole. Guaranteed!

3. The sketch **Tangent Circles.gsp** in the **Ellipse** folder shows a red circle c_3 that's simultaneously tangent to circles c_1 and c_2. Press the *Animate* button and observe the path of point *C*, the center of circle c_3. Can you prove that *C* traces an ellipse?

Exploring Conic Sections with The Geometer's Sketchpad
© 2002 Key Curriculum Press

The Congruent Triangles Construction   Name(s): _____

A **linkage** is any device with hinged and slotted rods.

The picture below appears in a book by the seventeenth-century mathematician Frans van Schooten. It shows a *linkage* consisting of three movable rods hinged together. In this activity, you'll explore a Sketchpad model of van Schooten's device and prove that it draws ellipses.

1. Open the sketch **Congruent Triangles.gsp** in the **Ellipse** folder. You'll see a construction that matches most of van Schooten's picture.

This sketch was created so that two equalities always hold. These are:

$$AB = FC$$
$$BF = CA$$

2. Drag point *C*. As you do, observe how the color-coded segments remain fixed in size and equal to each other.

3. Select point *E* and choose **Trace Intersection** from the Display menu. Drag point *C* and observe the curve traced by point *E*.

4. You've drawn what looks like half an ellipse. To trace the other half, use Sketchpad's **Reflect** command to reflect point *E* across segment *AB*. Select the reflected point, *E′*, and choose **Trace Point**. Now drag point *C* to trace the entire curve.

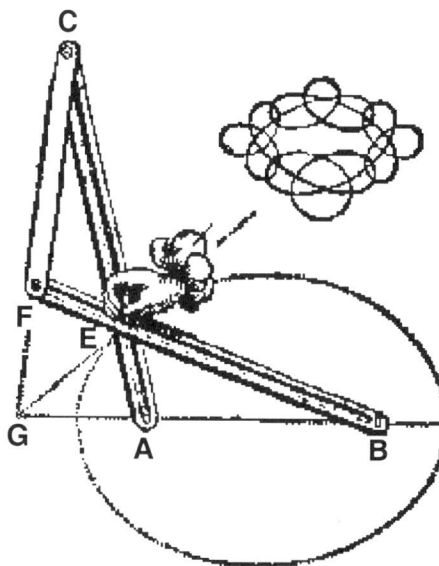

Questions

Q1 What appear to be the focal points of your ellipse?

Q2 The blue segment at the top left of your screen controls the lengths of segments *AB* and *FC*. Drag one of its endpoints to lengthen or shorten it. Choose **Erase Traces** from the Display menu to remove your previous curve. Now, retrace your curve. Do this several times.

How does the length of the blue segment affect your curve?

Q3 If you look at van Schooten's picture, you'll see that it includes a point *G*. Construct lines through segments *AB* and *FC* on your sketch so they meet at point *G*. Now draw a line through points *E* and *G*. Drag point *C*.

What is the relationship between this newly created line and your curve?

The Congruent Triangles Construction (continued)

How to Prove It

It certainly looks like the Congruent Triangles construction draws ellipses, but can you explain why? Try developing a proof on your own, or work through the following questions.

Questions

Q4 Add segment AF to your sketch. Using a triangle congruence theorem, show that $\triangle ABF \cong \triangle FCA$.

Q5 Use the result from the question above to complete this statement:

$$\angle FCA = \angle \underline{\hspace{2cm}}$$

Q6 Use the angle equality above and other information you know about the linkage to show that $\triangle AEB \cong \triangle FEC$.

Remember: An ellipse is the set of points such that the sum of the distances from each point to two fixed points (the foci) is constant.

→ **Q7** Segment AE is equal in length to which other segment? Why?

Q8 Use the distance definition of an ellipse and the result from Q7 to prove that point E traces an ellipse.

Explore More

1. This construction is sometimes called the *crossed parallelogram*. Explain why.

2. Use Sketchpad's **Trace** command to display the locus of point C as you drag it. Describe all of the similarities you can find between this sketch and the Folded Circle construction.

3. Open the sketch **Gears.gsp** in the **Ellipse** folder to operate a pair of elliptic gears.

You'll need to make liberal use of Sketchpad's **Circle by Center+Radius** command.

→ 4. Starting with a blank sketch, build your own Sketchpad model of the Congruent Triangles construction.

The Carpenter's Construction

Name(s): _____

The device pictured at right, a favorite among carpenters and woodworkers, is called an *ellipsograph* or *trammel*.

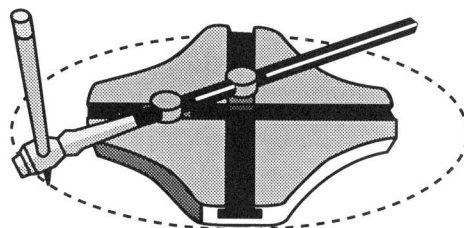

The ellipsograph first appears in the work of Proclus (A.D. 410–485).

An ellipsograph has an arm with two bolts that slide along a pair of perpendicular tracks. As the bolts glide along their respective grooves, a pen attached to one end draws an ellipse.

In this activity, you'll build your own ellipsograph with a ruler, then explore a more robust model with Sketchpad. Finally, you'll prove that this device really does draw ellipses.

Constructing a Physical Model

Preparation: You'll need a ruler, some masking tape, a pen or pencil, and a large piece of paper (11″×17″ is good, but 8.5″ ×11″ works also).

If you're working in a class, have members pick different placements of *B* relative to *A* and *C*. If you're working alone, do this activity twice with different point *B* locations.

1. Put a long strip of masking tape on a ruler, lining up an edge of the tape with an edge of the ruler. Mark three points, *A*, *B*, and *C*, on the tape. Make sure the distance between points *A* and *C* is less than half the width of your paper.

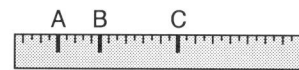

2. Use your ruler to draw a pair of perpendicular lines on the paper.

The illustration on the next page shows how to slide your ruler along the lines.

3. Begin by positioning point *B* at the intersection of the two lines and point *A* on the horizontal line to the left of *B*. Place a mark on your paper at point *C* (also on the horizontal line for now).

4. Slide the ruler just a little so that point *A* continues to lie on the horizontal line and point *B* lies on the vertical line. Mark the location of point *C*.

5. Continue to slide points *A* and *B* in small increments, keeping point *A* on the horizontal line and point *B* on the vertical line. Each time you reposition the ruler, mark point *C*'s position. Eventually the ruler will sit vertically with point *A* at the intersection point.

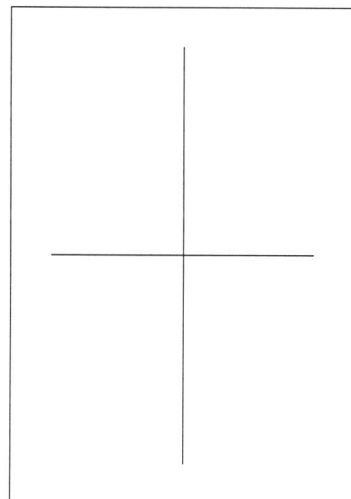

6. You've drawn what appears to be a quarter ellipse. Continue repositioning the ruler to draw the entire curve.

7. Discuss what you see with your classmates and compare their curves to yours. If you're doing this activity alone, draw a new curve by changing the location of point *B*.

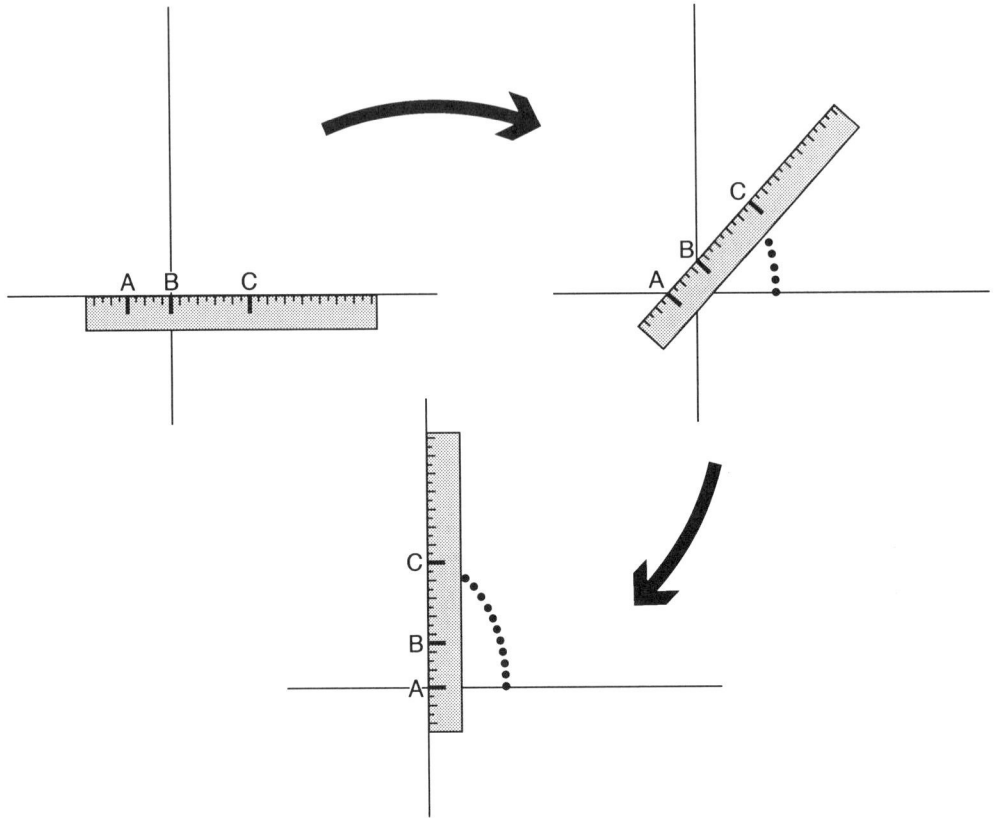

Questions

Q1 Shown below are two rulers with different relative locations for points *A*, *B*, and *C*. If each ruler is used to draw an ellipse, how will the shape of the two curves differ?

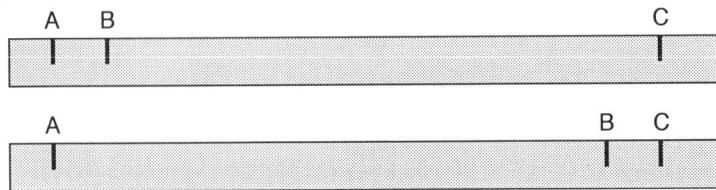

Q2 Assuming that ellipsographs do draw ellipses, how would you position points *A*, *B*, and *C* to draw an ellipse with a 20-cm major axis and a 12-cm minor axis?

Q3 Can an ellipsograph draw circles? Explain why or why not.

The Carpenter's Construction (continued)

Investigating a Sketchpad Model

Your ruler model of an ellipsograph provides a good sense of how the device works. Yet sliding the ruler bit by bit was probably awkward. A Sketchpad ellipsograph offers some advantages: a smooth, continuous motion and easily adjustable lengths.

8. Open the sketch **Carpenter.gsp** in the **Ellipse** folder.

9. Drag point A. As you do, watch the motion of segment AC.

10. Select point C and choose **Trace Intersection** from the Display menu. Drag point A and observe the curve traced by point C.

    The curve you see is the *locus* of point C as point A moves along its line.

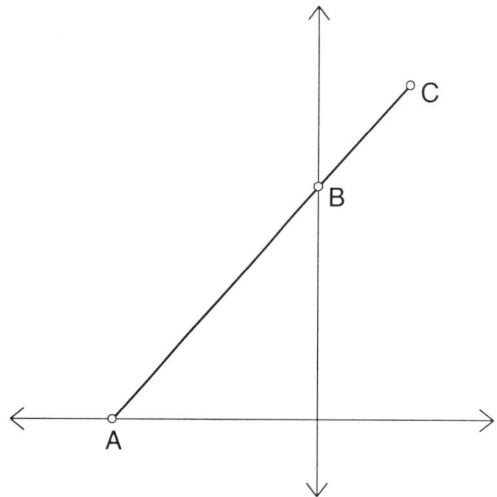

11. You've drawn what looks like half an ellipse. To trace the other half, use Sketchpad's **Reflect** command to reflect point C across the horizontal axis. Select the reflected point, C', and choose **Trace Point**. Now drag point A to trace the entire curve.

12. Adjust the lengths of $\overline{AB}$ and $\overline{BC}$ to vary the parameters of the ellipsograph. Then choose **Erase Traces** from the Display menu to erase your previous curve. Trace several new curves, each time varying the parameters AB and BC.

13. Turn tracing off for points C and C' by selecting them and once again choosing **Trace Points** from the Display menu.

14. Now select points A and C. Choose **Locus** from the Construct menu. Do this again for points A and C'. You'll form an entire curve: the locus of points C and C'.

15. As before, adjust the lengths of $\overline{AB}$ and $\overline{BC}$ to observe their effect on the curve.

How to Prove It

The curves you've drawn certainly *look* like ellipses. But appearances don't always tell the whole story. A proof can confirm the curves' identities and provide insights into the mathematics underlying ellipsographs.

Do you know the algebraic representation of an ellipse? Take a look at the following definition:

> *The points satisfying the equation*
>
> $$\frac{x^2}{a^2} + \frac{y^2}{b^2} = 1, \text{ with } b > a,$$
>
> *lie on an ellipse centered at the origin with major axis of length 2b along the y-axis and minor axis of length 2a along the x-axis.*

The illustration below shows an ellipsograph in the x-y plane whose arm is represented by segment AC. For this particular ellipsograph, $AB = 6$ and $BC = 3$. Several extra segments are included in the picture: segment CE is parallel to the y-axis and segment BD is parallel to the x-axis.

Since the location of point C changes as the ellipsograph's arm moves, it's labeled as (x, y), using variables as coordinates. If C traces an ellipse, you should be able to derive an equation like the one above relating x to y.

Questions

The questions that follow provide a step-by-step guided proof. You can answer them or write your own proof without any hints.

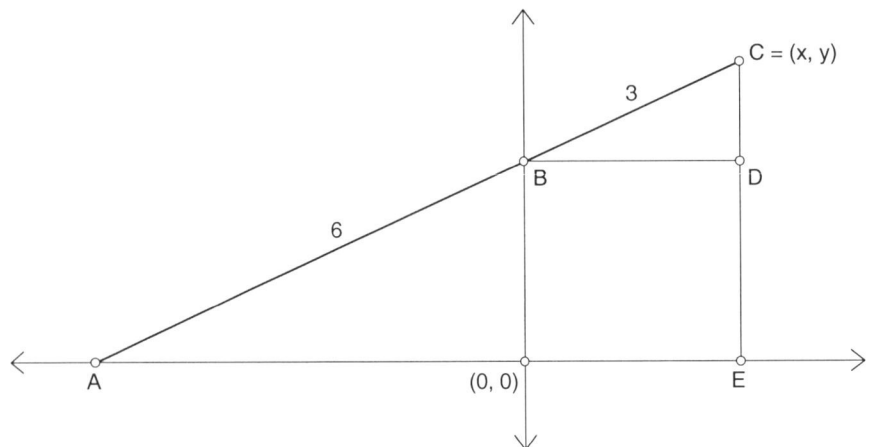

The Carpenter's Construction (continued)

Hint: Determine the lengths of the ellipse's major and minor axes, and the location of its center.

Q4 Assume for a moment—without proof—that the ellipsograph in the picture on the previous page draws an ellipse. Given that $AB = 6$ and $BC = 3$, what is its equation? (We'll compare our eventual answer with this equation later.)

Q5 Fill in the lengths of the following segments in terms of x and y:

$\overline{BD}$ = _____

$\overline{CE}$ = _____

$\overline{CD}$ = _____

Explain how you found the length of $\overline{CD}$.

Q6 Now that you've determined the lengths of various segments, find a way to relate x to y. Here are two approaches you might consider:

- Look for a pair of similar triangles in the diagram. Use their similarity to create a proportion relating x to y.
- Compute $\sin(\angle CAE)$ and $\cos(\angle CBD)$. Look for a way to relate these two values to each other.

If necessary, manipulate your equation so that it's recognizable as that of an ellipse. Compare your equation to the one you found in Q4 to see if they match.

Q7 Rewrite your proof, this time making it more general. Let $AB = s$ and $BC = t$.

Explore More

1. Starting with a blank sketch, build your own Sketchpad model of the ellipsograph construction.

Go to page 3 of **Carpenter.gsp** if you need help.

2. Given any curve drawn by an ellipsograph, you should be able to find its foci. Open page 2 of the sketch **Carpenter.gsp**. Use what you've learned in the Some Ellipse Relationships activity to construct the foci of the ellipse on screen.

Make sure your foci are *dynamic:* they should adjust to remain in the proper locations as you change the lengths of segments AB and BC.

The Carpenter's Construction (continued)

For added drama, imagine that *you're* standing on the ladder. What path does your foot trace?

3. The illustrations below show a seventeenth-century drawing device whose motion resembles that of a ladder sliding down a wall. On the ladder sits a bucket. As the ladder slides, what path does the bucket trace?

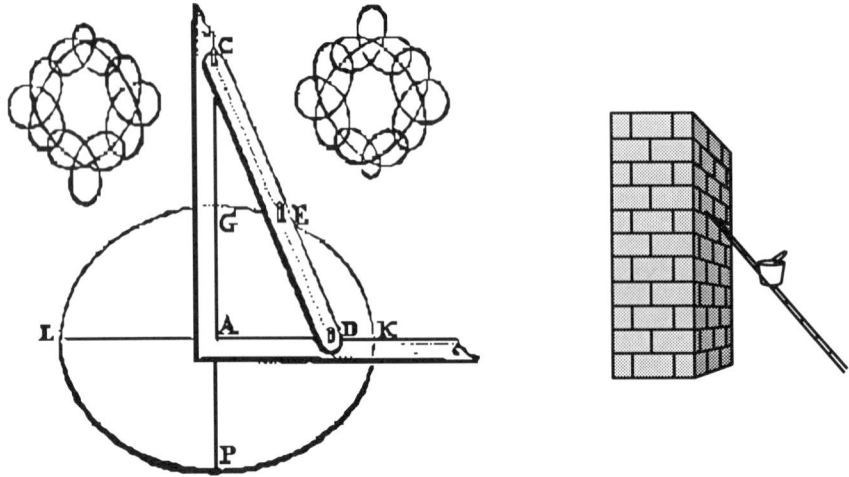

Investigate this problem by modifying your physical model of the ellipsograph. Build a Sketchpad model, too. Can you prove your findings?

4. There's a theorem from geometry that states:

> The midpoint of the hypotenuse of a right triangle is equidistant from the three vertices of the triangle.

Assume for the moment that this statement is true. How can you use it (and nothing else) to prove that the bucket from Q3 traces a circle when it's midway up the ladder?

5. Leonardo da Vinci devised an ellipse-tracing technique that substitutes a sliding triangle for the sliding ellipsograph.

Open the sketch **Triangle.gsp** in the **Ellipse** folder. Examine the path traced by triangle vertex *C* as the other two vertices slide along the *x*- and *y*-axes.

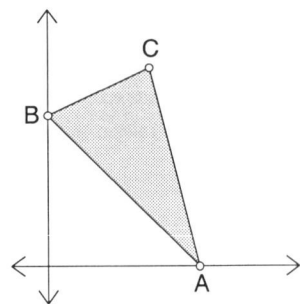

Danny's Ellipse

Name(s): _____

While a student at Mountain View High School in California, Danny Vizcaino devised a novel way to construct ellipses with Sketchpad. In this activity, you'll build a model of Danny's ellipse, then prove why his method works.

Constructing a Sketchpad Model

1. Open a new sketch. Choose **Show Grid** from the Graph menu. Then choose **Hide Grid** to remove the grid lines while keeping the *x*- and *y*-axes.

2. Label the origin (the intersection of the two lines) as point *A*.

3. Draw a random point *B* on the *y*-axis and a point *C* on the *x*-axis.

4. Select, in order, points *A* and *B*. Then choose **Circle by Center+Point** from the Construct menu to build a circle c_1 with center at point *A* passing through point *B*.

5. Repeat step 4 to construct a circle c_2 with center at point *A* passing through point *C*.

6. Draw a segment from point *A* to a random point *D* on circle c_2.

7. Construct point *E*, the intersection of segment *AD* with circle c_1.

8. Construct a line through point *D* perpendicular to the *x*-axis.

9. Construct a line through point *E* perpendicular to the *y*-axis.

10. Construct point *F*, the intersection of the two lines you just created.

11. Select point *F* and choose **Trace Intersection** from the Display menu. Drag point *D* around its circle and observe the curve traced by point *F*.

If you don't want your traces to fade, be sure the Fade Traces Over Time box is unchecked on the Color panel of the Preferences dialog box.

The curve you see is the *locus* of point *F* as point *D* moves around its circle.

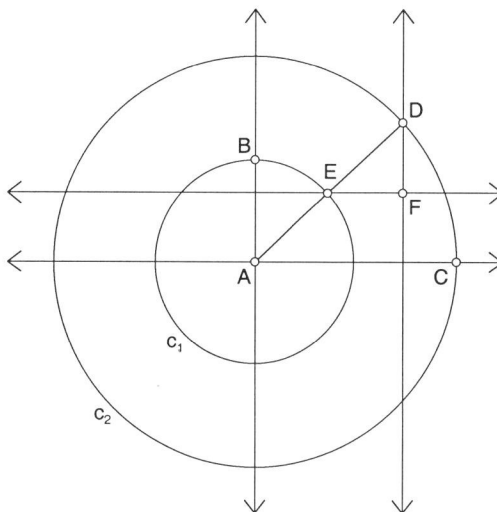

Danny's Ellipse (continued)

12. Drag points B and C to alter the sizes of circles c_1 and c_2. Then, if necessary, choose **Erase Traces** from the Display menu to erase your previous curve. Trace several new curves, each time varying the sizes of the two circles.

For every new location of points B and C, you need to retrace your curve. Ideally, your ellipse should adjust itself automatically. Sketchpad's powerful **Locus** command makes this possible.

13. Turn tracing off for point F by selecting it and once again choosing **Trace Intersection** from the Display menu.

14. Now select points D and F. Choose **Locus** from the Construct menu. You'll form an entire curve: the locus of point F. Drag points B and C to vary the shape of the curve.

How to Prove It

Open **Dynamic Geometry.gsp** in the **Ellipse** folder to see a fun application of Danny's method.

Intrigued by Danny's Sketchpad construction, Key Curriculum Press sponsored a worldwide contest to answer the following question:

Danny's curve *looks* like an ellipse, but is it?

The contest is over, but the challenge remains. Can you prove that Danny's curve is an ellipse? To do so, you'll need the algebraic definition below.

The points satisfying the equation

$$\frac{x^2}{a^2} + \frac{y^2}{b^2} = 1, \text{ with } a > b,$$

lie on an ellipse centered at the origin with major axis of length 2a along the x-axis and minor axis of length 2b along the y-axis.

In the illustration on the next page, $AE = 2$ and $ED = 3$. Segment EH is perpendicular to the x-axis. Since the location of point F changes as point D moves, it's labeled as (x, y), using variables as coordinates. If F traces an ellipse, you should be able to derive an equation like the one above relating x to y.

Danny's Ellipse (continued)

Questions

The questions that follow provide a step-by-step guided proof. You can answer them or write your own proof without any hints.

Q1 Assume for a moment— without proof—that Danny's curve is an ellipse. What is its equation? (We'll compare our eventual answer with this equation later.)

Hint: Determine the lengths of the ellipse's major and minor axes and the location of its center.

For Q1 and Q2, use the numerical values in the picture: $AE = 2$ and $ED = 3$.

Q2 Fill in the lengths of the following segments in terms of x and y:

$$\overline{AG} = \underline{\hphantom{XXXX}}$$

$$\overline{EH} = \underline{\hphantom{XXXX}}$$

$$\overline{DG} = \underline{\hphantom{XXXX}}$$

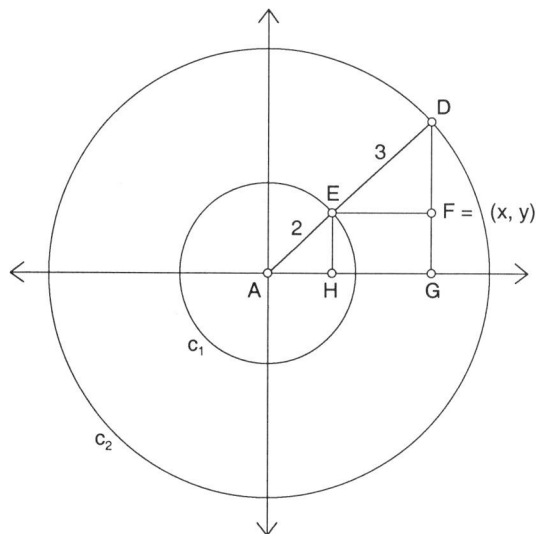

Explain how you found the length of $\overline{DG}$.

Q3 Now that you've determined the lengths of various segments, find a way to relate x to y. Here are two approaches you might consider:

- Look for a pair of similar triangles in the diagram. Use their similarity to create a proportion relating x to y.
- Compute $\sin(\angle EAH)$ and $\cos(\angle DAG)$. Look for a way to relate these two values to each other.

If necessary, manipulate your equation so that it's recognizable as that of an ellipse. Compare your equation to the one you found in Q1 to see if they match.

Q4 Rewrite your proof, this time making it more general. Let $AE = s$ and $ED = t$.

Explore More

See page 3 of **Danny.gsp** for help.

1. Since Danny's curve is an ellipse, you should be able to find its foci. Open the second page of the sketch **Danny.gsp** in the **Ellipse** folder. Use what you've learned in the Some Ellipse Relationships activity to construct the foci of the ellipse on screen.

   Make sure your foci are *dynamic:* they should adjust to remain in the proper locations as you drag point B or C.

Ellipse Projects

The projects below extend your ellipse knowledge in new directions and are ideal for in-class presentations.

1. Recall the distance definition of an ellipse:

    > An ellipse is the set of point P such that $PA + PB$ is constant for two fixed points, A and B.

    Suppose we define a new curve with a similar description:

    > The set of points P such that $PA + 2PB$ is constant for two fixed points, A and B.

    What does this curve look like? Build a Sketchpad model by modifying the Concentric Circles construction.

2. Open the sketch **Rhombus.gsp** in the **Ellipse** folder. You'll see the Folded Circle construction with one part missing—the crease line formed when point C is folded onto point B. You built this line by constructing the perpendicular bisector of segment BC.

    Imagine now that Sketchpad's **Perpendicular Line** and **Midpoint** commands are broken. How can you construct the crease line without them?

    Play with the completed sketch on page 3 of Rhombus.gsp so you'll understand how the linkage operates.

    The picture that follows offers one possibility. It's from the seventeenth-century mathematician Frans van Schooten and shows a rhombus $FCGB$ with a slotted rod passing through points F and G.

    How is this model similar to the Folded Circle construction? What purpose does the rhombus serve? Complete your sketch using a rhombus.

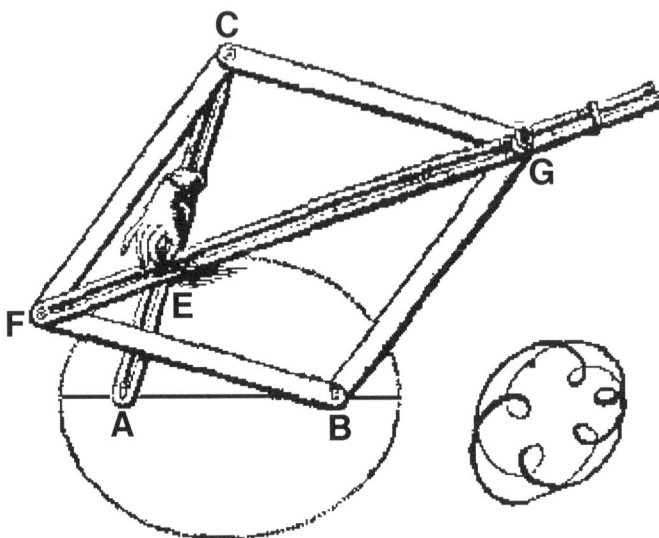

Ellipse Projects (continued)

3. The book *Feynman's Lost Lecture: The Motion of Planets Around the Sun* (W. W. Norton & Company, 2000) features a lecture by legendary physicist Richard Feynman. In his talk, Feynman uses the Folded Circle construction to demonstrate geometrically that planets orbit the sun in elliptic paths. Read Feynman's lecture and prepare a report on his method.

4. Build your own working model of the Congruent Triangles construction using cardboard and paper fasteners.

What happens when AB ≠ BC? → 5. Open the multi-page sketch **Bent Straw.gsp** in the **Ellipse** folder. You'll see a linkage with equal-length segments *AB* and *BC*. As you drag point *C*, notice how the motion of this device resembles that of a bent straw.

Can you prove point *D* traces an ellipse? The third page of the sketch contains some suggestions to get you started.

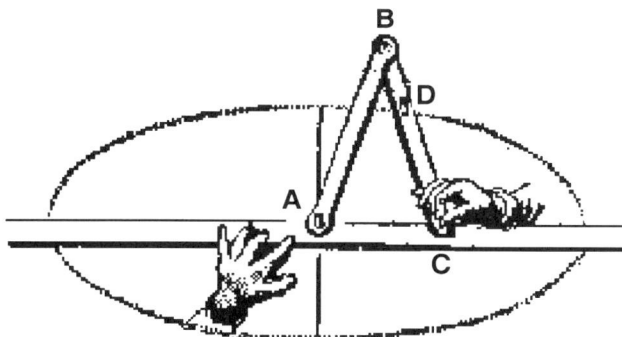

You'll use this tool in the Burning Tent activity later in this book. → 6. Use techniques from the Some Ellipse Relationships activity as well as from Danny's Ellipse to build a custom tool that takes three points—*A*, *B*, and *P*—and constructs an ellipse passing through *P* with *A* and *B* as foci.

If you need help, the sketch **Foci/Point.gsp** in the **Ellipse** folder provides assistance.

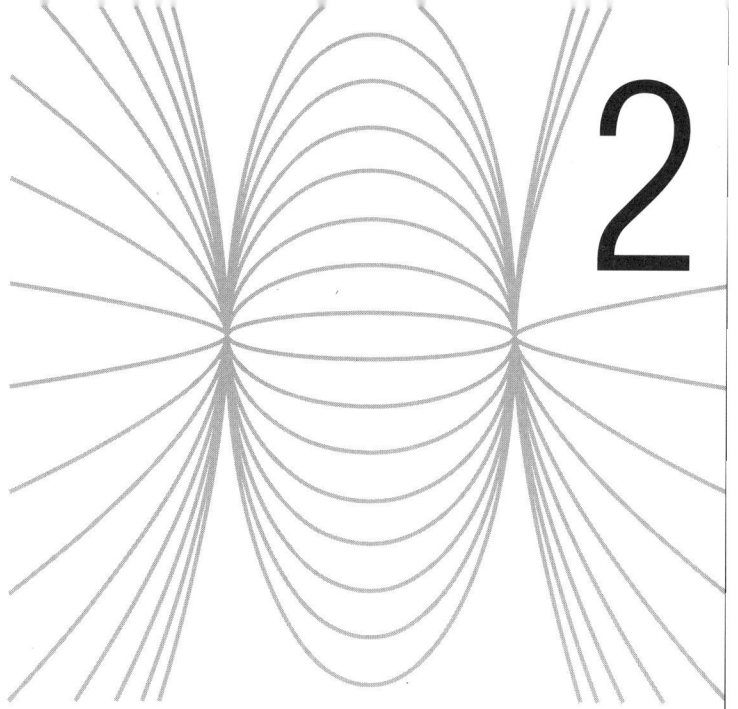

Parabolas

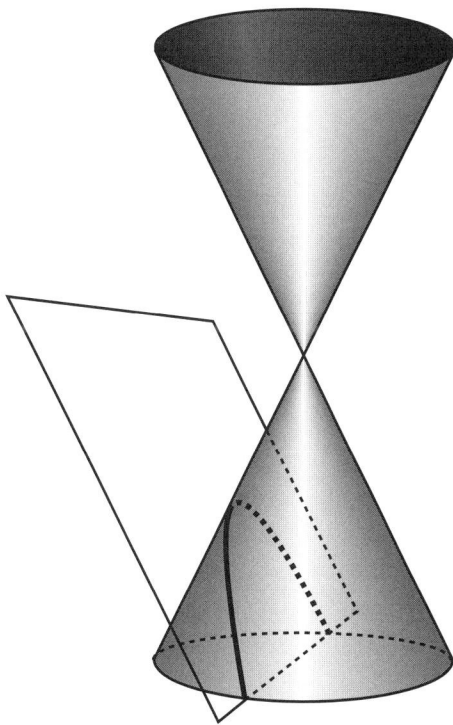

CHAPTER OVERVIEW

The path of a baseball. The curve formed by the cables on the Golden Gate Bridge. The trail of water jetting out from a hose. All of these are examples of parabolic curves (or very nearly so).

The picture at right shows a cone that's been sliced by a plane parallel to a side. The cross section (the "conic section") is a parabola.

This chapter opens with a look at a parabola's focus and directrix (activity I). It then presents two parabola constructions, one based on the parabola's distance definition (activity II) and the other on a parabola's algebraic form (activity III).

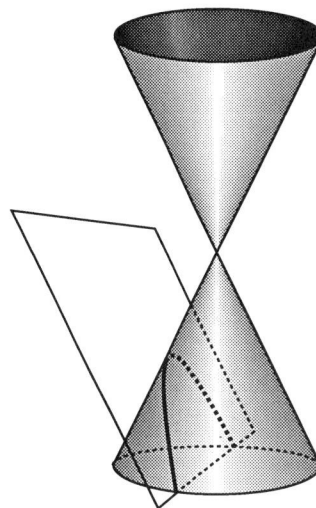

When a double-cone is cut by a plane that's parallel to an edge, the result is a *parabola*.

In total, this chapter offers seven parabola constructions for you to sample. Open the multi-page sketch **Parabola Tour.gsp** for a handy slide-show overview.

I. Introducing the Parabola

A focal point and a directrix line are the main ingredients for two parabola constructions.

II. The Folded Rectangle Construction

With just a blank sheet of paper and a single point, you can fold yourself a genuine parabola. Model the technique with Sketchpad to reveal the underlying mathematics.

III. The Expanding Circle Construction

As a circle grows and shrinks, it defines points that lie along a parabola. Investigate this tenth-century construction with the aid of Sketchpad.

IV. Parabola Projects

Round out the chapter with some pleasing parabola projects.

Introducing the Parabola

Name(s): _____

In this activity, the geometric definition of a parabola serves as a gateway for investigating two different ways to construct the curve.

Defining a Parabola

Below is the geometric definition of a parabola:

> *A **parabola** is the set of points equidistant from a fixed point (the **focus**) and a fixed line (the **directrix**).*

If you open the sketch **Parabola.gsp** in the **Parabola** folder, you'll see a parabola along with its focus and directrix. The sketch also contains two measurements showing the distance of point P from the focus and from the directrix.

Drag point P. You'll see the distance measurements change, but always remain equal to each other.

The parabola is a symmetric curve. Its line of symmetry passes through the focus and through a point called the **vertex**. In the parabola below, the vertex is the lowest point on the curve.

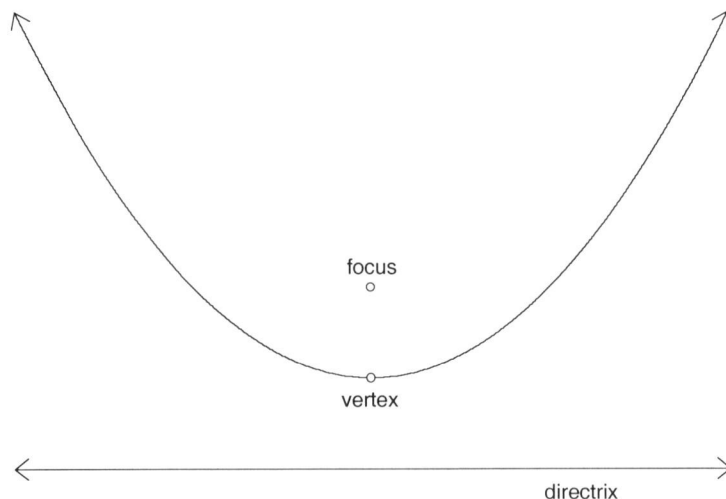

focus
○

○
vertex

directrix

Questions

Q1 Given a line d and a point P not on the line, how do we define the distance between them?

Alternatively, press the *show segments* button.

Q2 Draw a segment from point P to the focus. Then construct a segment whose length represents the distance from point P to the directrix. The segments should adjust themselves as point P moves along the parabola.

Use Sketchpad to measure the lengths of these two segments. What do you expect to find?

Q3 Given just a parabola's focus and directrix, how can you construct its vertex?

The Concentric Circles Method

Concentric circles share the same center.

The illustration below shows nine concentric circles centered at point *A*. The radii of the circles increase by 1's, from 1 unit all the way up to 9 units. The horizontal lines are also spaced 1 unit apart. Each line, except the one passing through point *A*, is tangent to a circle.

We can use this arrangement to draw parabolas.

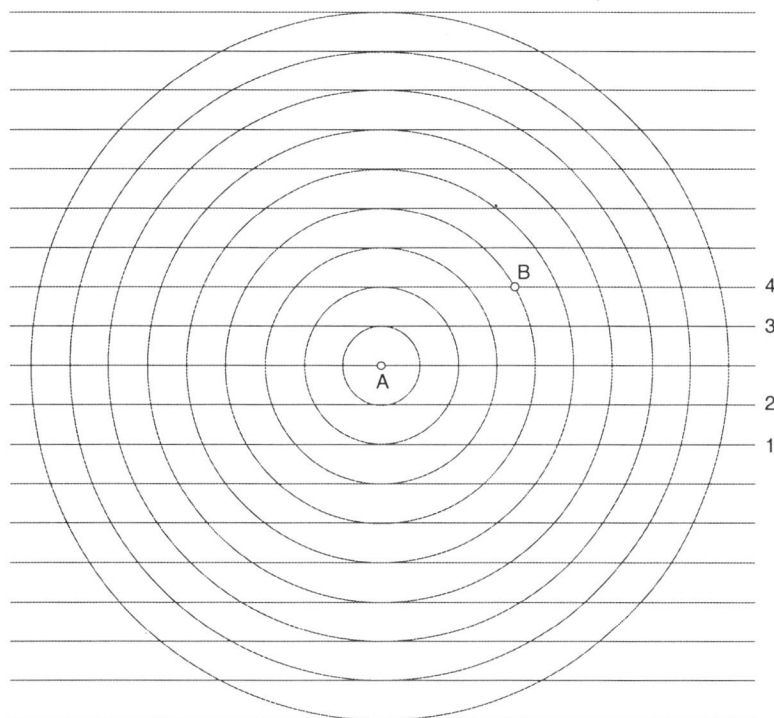

Questions

Q4 How many units apart are points *A* and *B*? How many units apart are point *B* and line 1? Based on these measurements, what can you conclude?

Q5 Locate and mark at least 15 points (including the vertex) that sit on a parabola with focal point at *A* and line 1 as its directrix. Explain how you found them.

Q6 Using the points you found as guidelines, sketch the parabola.

Q7 Repeat the previous two questions, drawing parabolas with directrix lines 2, 3, and 4. All three parabolas will have *A* as their focal point. For each parabola, use a different colored pen or pencil if possible.

The Sliding Ruler Method

Open the sketch **Sliding Ruler.gsp** in the **Parabola** folder. You'll see the model below.

The rectangles represent two rulers. A piece of string equal in length to *BD* is attached from point *A* to the corner of the vertical ruler (point *B*). The string is held taut against the edge of the ruler by a pencil at point *C*.

Sliding ruler *BD* to the right while keeping the string taut causes point *C* to trace half a parabola.

To operate the Sketchpad model, drag point *D*.

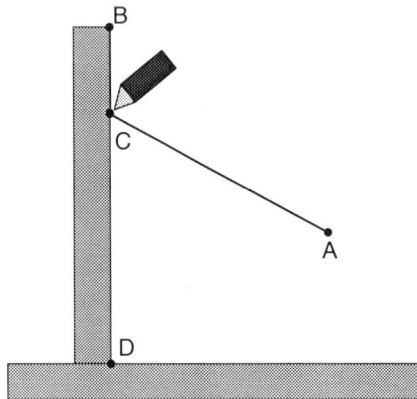

How to Prove It

The Sliding Ruler construction seems to draw parabolas. Can you prove that it does? Try developing a proof on your own or work through the following questions.

Questions

Q8 Assuming the pencil at point *C* traces a parabola, where are the focus and directrix?

Q9 Assuming the pencil at point *C* traces a parabola, which two segments must you prove equal in length?

Remember: The length of string is equal to the length of ruler BD.

Q10 Complete this statement:

$$BC + CA = BC + \underline{\hspace{2cm}}$$

Q11 Complete the proof.

Explore More

1. Circles come in different sizes, but all circles share the same shape. Given any two circles, you can enlarge or reduce one circle on a photocopy machine so that it matches the other.

   Believe it or not, all parabolas possess the same property: Given any two, it's possible to enlarge or reduce one parabola on a photocopy machine so that it matches the other.

   Not convinced? Open the sketch **Scale.gsp** in the **Parabola** folder. Two parabolas appear onscreen—one red, one green. Drag the unit point "1" on the x-axis. The green parabola will stay in place, but the red parabola will adjust to the change of scale on the x- and y-axes.

   Because the scaling on the two axes grows and shrinks in unison, the equation of the red parabola ($y = x^2$) doesn't change. By dragging the unit point, you should be able to make the two parabolas overlap.

The Folded Rectangle Construction   Name(s): _____

With nothing more than a sheet of paper and a single point on the page, you can create a parabola. No rulers and no measuring required!

Constructing a Physical Model

> **Preparation:** You'll need a rectangular or square piece of wax paper or patty paper. If you don't have these materials, use a plain sheet of paper.

If you're working in a class, have members place A at different distances from the edge. If you're working alone, do this section twice—once with A close to the edge, once with A farther from the edge.

1. Mark a point A approximately one inch from the bottom of the paper and centered between the left and right edges.

2. As shown below right, fold the paper so that a point on the bottom edge lands directly onto point A. Make a sharp crease to keep a record of this fold. Unfold the crease.

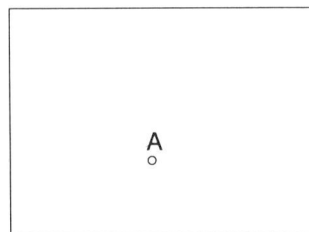

3. Fold the paper along a new crease so that a different point on the bottom edge lands on point A. Unfold the crease and repeat the process.

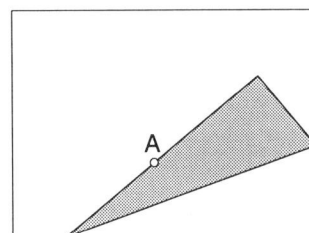

4. After you've made a dozen or so creases, examine them to see if you spot any emerging patterns.

*Mathematicians would describe your set of creases as an **envelope** of creases.*

5. Resume creasing the paper. Gradually, you should see a well-outlined curve appear. Be patient—it may take a little while.

6. Discuss what you see with your classmates and compare their folded curves to yours. If you're doing this activity alone, fold a second sheet of paper with point A farther from the bottom edge.

Questions

Q1 The creases on your paper seem to form the outline of a parabola. Where do its focus and directrix appear to be?

Q2 If you were to move point A closer to the bottom edge of the paper and fold another curve, how do you think its shape would compare to the first curve?

Exploring Conic Sections with The Geometer's Sketchpad
© 2002 Key Curriculum Press

The Folded Rectangle Construction (continued)

Constructing a Sketchpad Model

Fold and unfold. Fold and unfold. Creasing your paper takes some work. Folding one or two sheets is fun, but what would happen if you wanted to continue testing many different locations for point *A*? You'd need to keep starting over with fresh paper, folding new sets of creases.

Sketchpad can streamline your work. With just one set of creases, you can drag point *A* to new locations and watch the crease lines adjust themselves instantaneously.

7. Open a new sketch. Use the **Line** tool to draw a horizontal line near the bottom of the screen. This line represents the bottom edge of the paper.

8. Draw a point *A* above the line, roughly centered between the left and right edges of the screen.

9. Construct a point *B* on the horizontal line.

10. Construct the "crease" formed when point *B* is folded onto point *A*.

11. Drag point *B* along its line. If you constructed your crease line correctly, it should adjust to the new locations of point *B*.

If you don't want your traces to fade, be sure the Fade Traces Over Time box is unchecked on the Color panel of the Preferences dialog box.

12. Select the crease line and choose **Trace Line** from the Display menu.

13. Drag point *B* along the horizontal line to create a collection of crease lines.

14. Drag point *A* to a different location, then, if necessary, choose **Erase Traces** from the Display menu.

15. Drag point *B* to create another collection of crease lines.

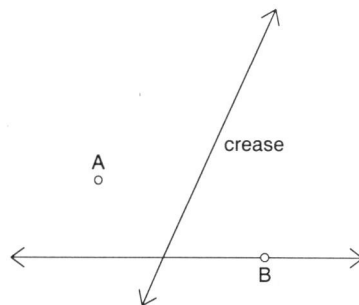

Retracing creases for each location of point *A* is certainly faster than folding paper. But we can do better. Ideally, your crease lines should relocate automatically as you drag point *A*. Sketchpad's powerful **Locus** command makes this possible.

16. Turn tracing off for your original crease line by selecting it and once again choosing **Trace Line** from the Display menu.

17. Now select your crease line and point *B*. Choose **Locus** from the Construct menu. An entire set of creases will appear: the locus of crease locations as point *B* moves along its path. If you drag point *A*, you'll see that the crease lines readjust automatically.

Questions

Q3 How does the appearance of the curve change as you move point *A* closer to the horizontal line?

Q4 How does the appearance of the curve change as you move point *A* away from the horizontal line?

Playing Detective

Each crease line on your paper touches the parabola at exactly one point. Another way of saying this is that each crease is *tangent* to the parabola. By engaging in some detective work, you can locate these tangency points and use them to construct just the parabola without its creases.

18. Open the sketch **Folded Rectangle.gsp** in the **Parabola** folder. You'll see a thick crease line and its locus already in place.

19. Drag point *B* and notice that the crease line remains tangent to the parabola. The exact point of tangency lies at the intersection of two lines—the crease line and another line not shown here. Construct this line in your sketch as well as the point of tangency, point *D*.

Select the locus and make its width thicker so that it's easier to see. →

20. Select point *D* and point *B* and choose **Locus** from the Construct menu. If you've constructed point *D* correctly, you should see a curve appear precisely in the white space bordered by the creases.

How to Prove It

The Folded Rectangle construction seems to generate parabolas. Can you prove that it does? Try developing a proof on your own or work through the following steps and questions.

The picture below should resemble your Sketchpad construction. Line *EF* (the perpendicular bisector of segment *AB*) represents the crease line formed when point *B* is folded onto point *A*. Point *D* sits on the curve itself.

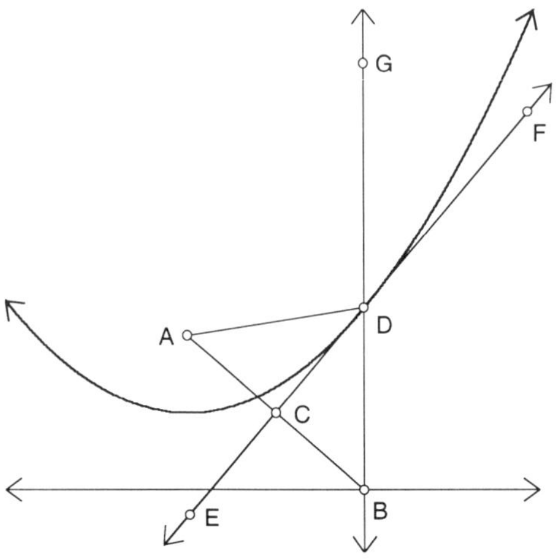

Questions

Q5 Assuming point D traces a parabola, which two segments must you prove equal in length?

Q6 Use a triangle congruence theorem to prove that $\triangle ACD \cong \triangle BCD$.

Remember, a parabola is the set of points equidistant from a fixed point (the focus) and a fixed line (the directrix).

→ **Q7** Use the distance definition of a parabola and the result from Q6 to prove that point D traces a parabola.

Explore More

1. Open the sketch **Tangent Circle.gsp** in the **Parabola** folder. You'll see a circle with center at point C that passes through point A and is tangent to a line at point B. Drag point B. Why does point C trace a parabola?

2. A parabola can be described as an ellipse with one focal point at infinity.

   Open the sketch **Conic Connection.gsp** in the **Parabola** folder. You'll see the ellipse and circle from the Folded Circle construction. Press the *send focal point to "infinity"* button. Point A—a focal point of the ellipse and the center of the circle—will travel far off the screen.

   When the movement stops, examine the result. In what ways does it resemble the Folded Rectangle construction?

3. Use the illustration from your parabola proof to show that $\angle GDF = \angle ADC$. The sketch **Headlights.gsp** in the **Parabola** folder illustrates a nice consequence of this result.

The Expanding Circle Construction   Name(s): _____

In this activity, you'll explore a little-known parabola construction from the tenth century. The method originates from Ibn Sina, a jack-of-all-trades who was a physician, philosopher, mathematician, *and* astronomer!

Constructing a Sketchpad Model

1. Open a new sketch. Choose **Show Grid** from the Graph menu. Then choose **Hide Grid** to remove the grid lines while keeping the *x*- and *y*-axes.

2. Label the origin as point *A*.

3. Choose the **Compass** tool. Click on the *y*-axis above the origin (point *C*) and then below the origin (point *B*). You'll create a circle with center at point *C* passing through point *B*.

4. Construct point *D*, the intersection of the circle and the positive *y*-axis.

5. Construct points *E* and *F*, the intersections of the circle and the *x*-axis.

6. Construct lines through points *E* and *F* perpendicular to the *x*-axis.

7. Construct a line through point *D* perpendicular to the *y*-axis.

8. Construct points *G* and *H*, the intersections of the three newly created lines.

9. Select points *G* and *H* and choose **Trace Intersections** from the Display menu. Drag point *C* up and down the *y*-axis and observe the curve traced by points *G* and *H*.

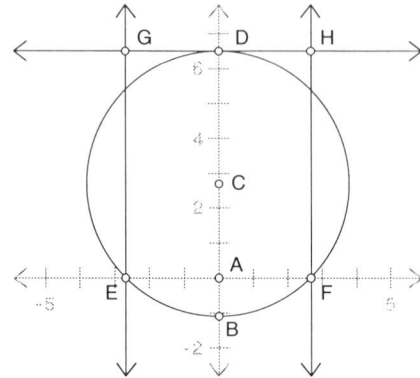

   The curve you see is the *locus* of points *G* and *H* as point *C* travels along the *y*-axis.

10. Drag point *B* to a new location, but keep it below the origin. Then, if necessary, choose **Erase Traces** from the Display menu to erase your previous curve. Trace several new curves, each time changing the location of point *B*.

For every new location of point *B*, you need to retrace your curve. Ideally, your parabola should adjust automatically as you drag point *B*. Sketchpad's powerful **Locus** command makes this possible.

11. Turn tracing off for points *G* and *H* by selecting them and once again choosing **Trace Intersections** from the Display menu.

12. Now select points *G* and *C*. Choose **Locus** from the Construct menu. Do this again for points *H* and *C*. You'll form an entire curve: the locus of points *G* and *H*. Drag point *B* to vary the shape of the curve.

Questions

Q1 As you drag point *B*, which features of the curve stay the same? Which features change?

Q2 The creator of this technique, Ibn Sina, didn't, of course, have Sketchpad available to him in the tenth century! How would this construction be different if you used a compass and straightedge instead?

The Geometric Mean

It certainly looks like the Expanding Circle method draws parabolas, but to prove why, you'll need to know a little about *geometric means*.

> The **geometric mean** x of two numbers, a and b, is equal to $\sqrt{ab}$.
>
> Equivalently, $x^2 = ab$.

Thus the geometric mean of 4 and 9 is

$$\sqrt{(4)(9)} = 6$$

It's possible to determine the geometric mean of two numbers geometrically rather than algebraically. Specifically, if two segments have lengths *a* and *b*, we can construct—without measuring—a third segment of length $\sqrt{ab}$.

13. Open the sketch **Geometric Mean.gsp** in the **Parabola** folder.

    You'll see a circle whose diameter consists of two segments with lengths *a* and *b* laid side to side. A chord perpendicular to the diameter is split into equal segments of length *x*.

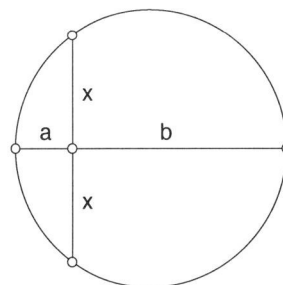

14. Use Sketchpad's calculator to compute the geometric mean of lengths *a* and *b*. Compare this value to *x*.

The Expanding Circle Construction (continued)

Questions

Q3 The second page of **Geometric Mean.gsp** outlines a proof showing that x is the geometric mean of a and b. Complete the proof.

How to Prove It

With your knowledge of geometric means, you can now prove that points G and H of the Expanding Circle construction trace a parabola.

Since the location of point H changes as the circle grows and shrinks, it's labeled below as (x, y), using variables as coordinates. To make things more concrete, we'll assume $AB = 3$.

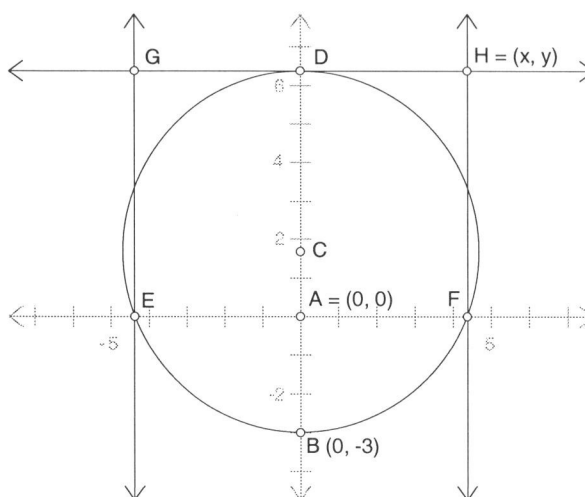

Questions

The questions that follow provide a step-by-step guided proof. You can answer them or first write your own proof without any hints.

Q4 Fill in the lengths of the following segments in terms of x and y:

$\overline{AF} = $ _____

$\overline{AD} = $ _____

Q5 Use your knowledge of geometric means to write an equation relating the lengths of $\overline{AB}$, $\overline{AF}$, and $\overline{AD}$. Is this the equation of a parabola?

Q6 Give an argument to explain why point G also traces a parabola.

Q7 Rewrite your proof, this time making it more general. Let $AB = s$.

Explore More

1. Open the sketch **Right Angle.gsp** in the **Parabola** folder. Angle DEB is constructed to be a right angle. Drag point E and observe the trace of point G and its reflection G'. Explain why this sketch is essentially the same as the Expanding Circle construction.

Parabola Projects

The projects below extend your parabola knowledge in new directions and are ideal for in-class presentations.

1. Build your own physical model of the Sliding Ruler construction.

2. Create a custom tool that automatically builds a parabola given a directrix and a focal point.

3. Open the sketch **Rhombus.gsp** in the **Parabola** folder. You'll see the Folded Rectangle construction with one part missing—the crease line formed when point *B* is folded onto point *A*. You built this line by constructing the perpendicular bisector of segment *AB*. Is there another way to do it?

Play with the completed sketch on page 3 of **Rhombus.gsp** so you'll understand how the linkage operates.

The picture that follows offers one possibility. It's from the seventeenth-century mathematician Frans van Schooten and shows a rhombus *EBFA* with a slotted rod passing through points *E* and *F*. (Look on the back cover for a working model of this linkage.)

How is this model similar to the Folded Rectangle construction? What purpose does the rhombus serve? Complete the sketch using a rhombus.

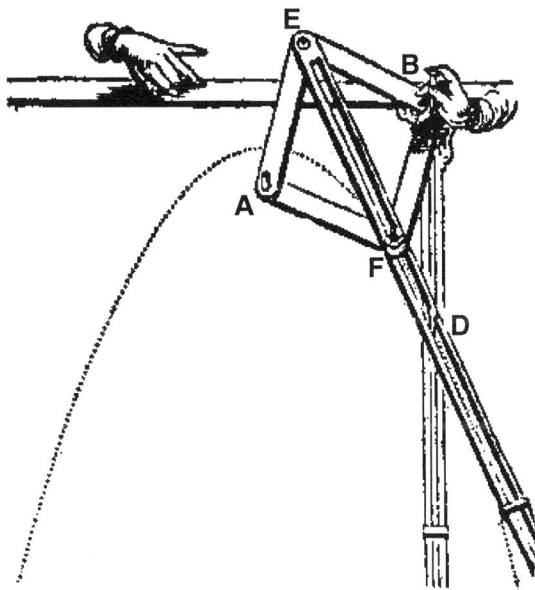

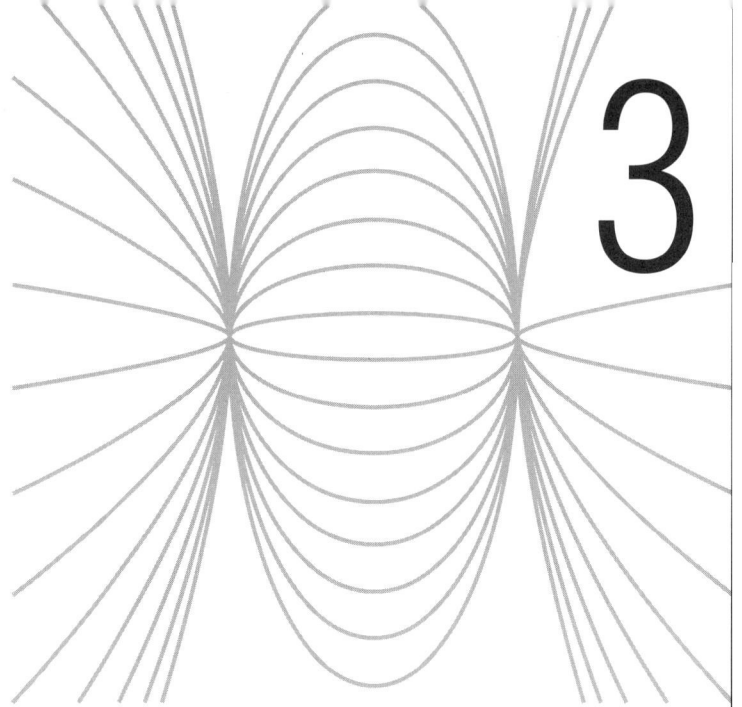

Hyperbolas

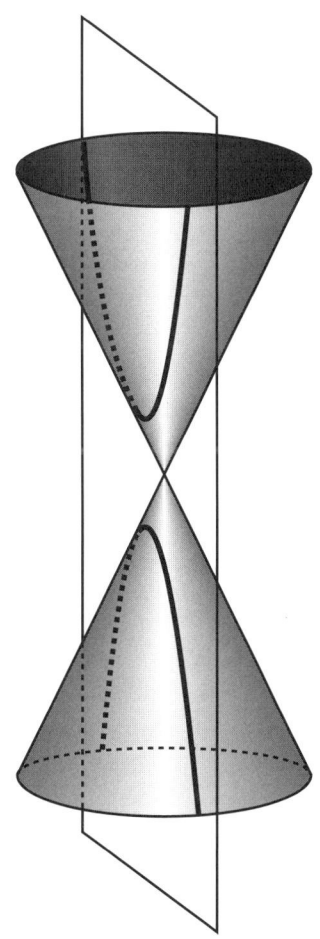

CHAPTER OVERVIEW

The shadows cast on a wall by a lamp with a cylindrical shade. The paths of comets that enter the inner solar system and then leave forever. The mirrors in many reflecting telescopes. All of these are examples of hyperbolic curves.

The picture at right shows a double cone being sliced by a plane. The cross section (the "conic section") is a hyperbola.

After an introduction to the distance definition of a hyperbola in activity I, a variety of hyperbola construction techniques are presented in activities II and III. In total, you'll find seven methods to sample. Open the multi-page sketch **Hyperbola Tour.gsp** for a handy slide-show overview.

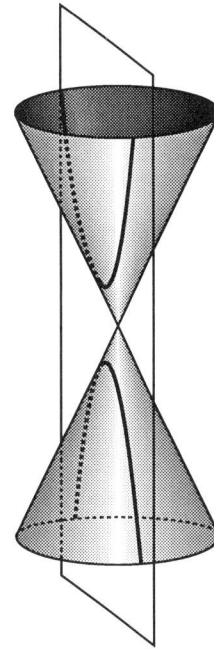

When a plane cuts both halves of a double-cone, the result is a *hyperbola*. The plane need not be parallel to the double-cone's axis.

I. Introducing the Hyperbola

Gold coins await the treasure seekers who successfully apply the distance definition of a hyperbola.

II. The Concentric Circles Construction

The distance definition of a hyperbola serves as a springboard for two hyperbola constructions: one built from concentric circles, the other from a rotating ruler.

III. Hyperbola Projects

Round out the chapter with more hyperbola goodies.

Introducing the Hyperbola

Name(s): _____

What does it take to find buried treasure? A map, a shovel—and would you believe a hyperbola or two? Yes, with nothing more than two hyperbolas, you can track down some hidden gold. You'll be on your way once you learn the definition of these curves.

What Is a Hyperbola?

Here is the geometric definition of a hyperbola:

> A **hyperbola** is the set of points P such that the difference of the distances from P to two fixed points (the **foci**) is constant.

If you open the sketch **Hyperbola.gsp** in the **Hyperbola** folder, you'll see a hyperbola along with its foci, F_1 and F_2. Every hyperbola consists of two separate branches. Point P currently sits on the left branch of the hyperbola.

For an ellipse, the *sum* of the distances from every point on the curve to the two foci remains constant. But for a hyperbola, it is the *difference* of the two distances that remains constant.

Of course, the difference of two numbers is either a positive or a negative number, depending on the order of subtraction. If you move point P along the left branch of the hyperbola, then drag it onto the right branch, you'll see that the value of $PF_2 - PF_1$ switches from positive to negative.

Dragging either focal point to a new location will change the value of this constant difference.

In a hyperbola, it is the *absolute value* of $PF_2 - PF_1$ that remains constant.

Every hyperbola also has two lines associated with it: the *asymptotes*. The two branches of the hyperbola approach these lines but never touch them. If you open page two of the sketch and press the Movement button, you can monitor the ever-shrinking distance between a hyperbola branch and its asymptote. If this animation could continue indefinitely, you'd see the distance value continue to approach zero, but never reach it.

'X' Marks the Spot

Legend has it that the island of Keypress contains a buried treasure chest of gold. After years of searching, you find the following note:

> My treasure is two miles farther away from the giant boulder (point B) than the lighthouse (point L). It's also three miles farther away from the cave (point C) than the jail (point J).

Open the sketch **Treasure.gsp** in the **Hyperbola** folder to view the landmarks in the note. Can you pinpoint the exact spot where the treasure is buried?

As help, the sketch contains two hyperbolas: one with foci at B and L, the other with foci at C and J. You can change the constant difference associated with each hyperbola by dragging the segments that sit along the left edge of the sketch.

Explain your method and why it works.

The Concentric Circles Construction Name(s): _____

Circles that are concentric share the same center. In this activity, you'll use two sets of concentric circles to draw a hyperbola by hand. You'll then transfer this technique to Sketchpad to draw a hyperbola whose shape and size can be adjusted by just dragging your mouse.

Sketching Hyperbolas by Hand

The illustration that follows shows two sets of concentric circles. One set of circles is centered at point F_1, the other at point F_2. For each set, the radii of the circles increase by 1's, from 1 unit all the way up to 7 units.

Points F_1 and F_2 are the foci of an infinite number of hyperbolas, but only two that we're interested in: one hyperbola that passes through point A and another that passes through point B.

Q1 How many units apart are points A and F_1? How many units apart are points A and F_2? What is the numerical value of $AF_1 - AF_2$?

Q2 Locate and mark at least 16 points that sit on either branch of the hyperbola passing through point A. Explain how you found them.

Q3 Locate and mark at least 16 points that sit on either branch of the hyperbola passing through point B. (Use a different colored pen or pencil if possible.) Explain how you found them.

Q4 Using the points you found as guidelines, sketch the two hyperbolas.

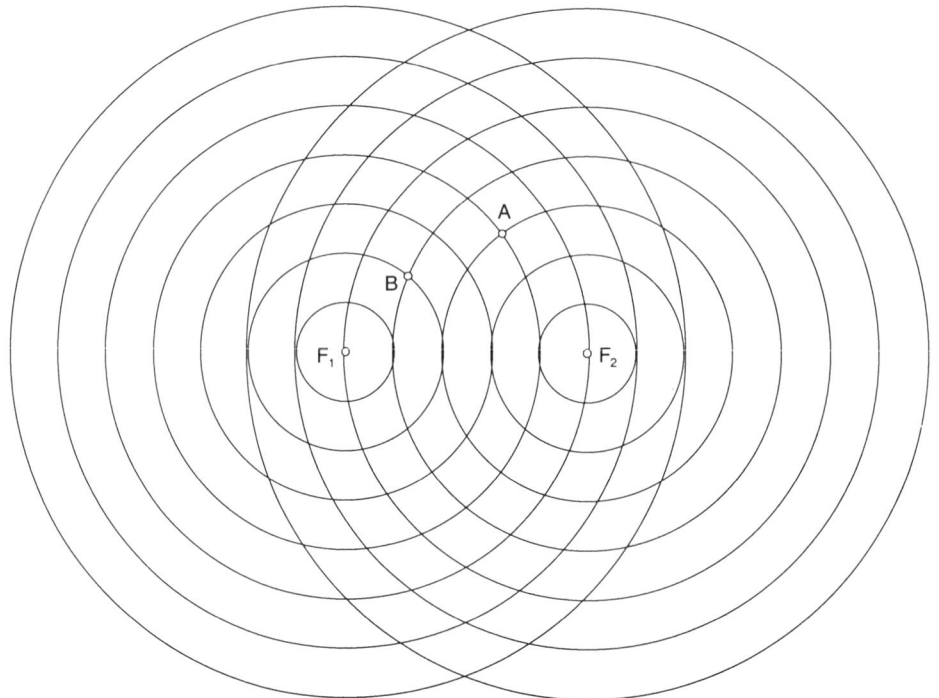

The Concentric Circles Construction (continued)

By dropping two stones into a peaceful pond, you can create an animated version of the concentric circles. Open the sketch **Ripples.gsp** in the **Hyperbola** folder and press the *Animate* button to view some ripples and their accompanying hyperbolas.

Examining a Sketchpad Model

Now that you've drawn some hyperbolas by hand, it's time to examine a dynamic one: a hyperbola that changes shape as its parts are dragged.

Open the sketch **Concentric Circles.gsp** in the **Hyperbola** folder. You'll see two circles—one red, one blue. The sizes of these two circles are controlled by the segments at the top of the screen. The red circle has radius AC and center F_1, the blue circle has radius BC and center F_1.

To operate this model, drag point C. As you do, the radii will adjust to remain equal to $\overline{AC}$ and $\overline{BC}$. At the same time, you'll be tracing the intersection points of the two circles.

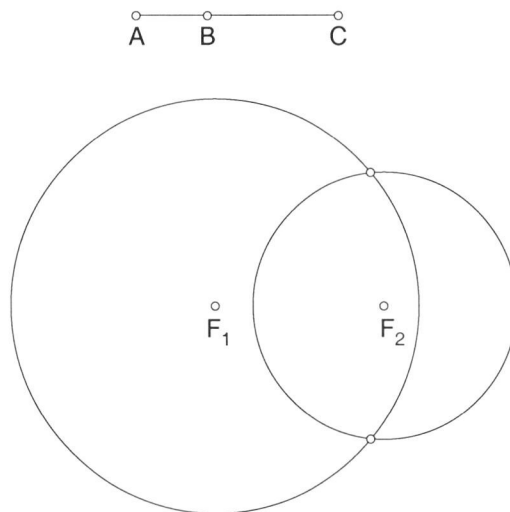

Drag point C to the right of point B, then back to the left of point A.

Questions

Q5 As you drag point C, the radii of both circles change lengths. Still, there is a relationship that exists between the two radii whenever point C is to the right of point B or to the left of point A. What is it?

Q6 Explain why the intersection points of the two circles trace a hyperbola.

Q7 Select your two onscreen circles, choose **Trace Circles** from the Display menu, then drag point C.

Based on this experiment, describe the similarities between your Sketchpad construction and the concentric circles technique.

The Rotating Ruler Method

Open the sketch **Rotating Ruler.gsp** in the **Hyperbola** folder. You'll see the model below.

The rectangle represents a ruler that rotates around the fixed point F_2. A string is attached from point F_1 to the corner of the ruler (point B). The string is held taut against the edge of the ruler by a pencil at point A.

Pulling the pencil up along the edge of the ruler causes the ruler to rotate while point A traces a piece of a hyperbola.

To operate the Sketchpad model, drag point B.

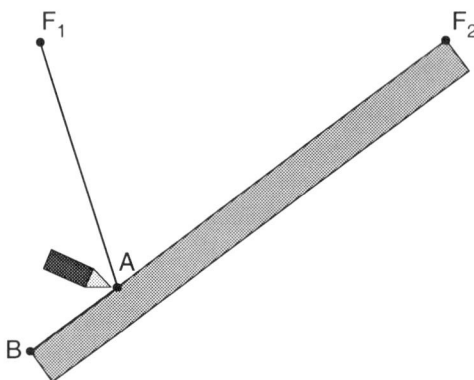

How to Prove It

Can you prove that the Rotating Ruler draws hyperbolas? Try developing a proof on your own or work through the following questions.

Questions

Q8 If the pencil at point A does indeed trace a hyperbola with foci at F_1 and F_2, then what value must you prove constant?

Q9 Explain why the following equality holds:

$$\left| (BA + AF_2) - (BA + AF_1) \right| = \text{constant}$$

Q10 Complete the proof.

Hyperbola Projects

The projects below extend your hyperbola knowledge in new directions and are ideal for in-class presentations.

1. In the Folded Circle Construction (Chapter 1) you picked a point *B* within a circle and then folded the circle repeatedly so that points on its circumference landed on *B*. The outline of creases formed an ellipse. If you've saved your sketch from that activity, open it. If not, open **Folded Circle Revisited.gsp** in the **Hyperbola** folder.

   What happens when point *B* sits outside the circle? Drag point *B* to find out. (You might want to model this construction with paper also—draw a circle on a sheet of notebook paper, mark a point *B* outside the circle, then fold point *B* repeatedly onto different points along the circumference.)

   Hint: In the Folded Circle Construction, you connected points *A* and *C* with a segment. Try something similar here.

   Can you prove that this modified construction generates hyperbolas? To do so, you'll need to find which point along each crease line is tangent to the hyperbola.

2. Open the sketch **Rhombus.gsp** in the **Hyperbola** folder. You'll see the construction from Project 1 above with one thing missing—the crease line formed when point *B* is folded onto point *C*. You built this line by constructing the perpendicular bisector of segment *BC*.

   Imagine that Sketchpad's **Perpendicular Line** and **Midpoint** commands are broken. Can you construct the crease without them?

   Play with the completed sketch on page 3 of **Rhombus.gsp** so you'll understand how the linkage operates.

   The linkage below from seventeenth-century mathematician Frans van Schooten offers one possibility. It shows a rhombus *FBGC* with a slotted rod passing through points *F* and *G*.

   What purpose does the rhombus serve? How is this model similar to that in Project 1? Complete your sketch using a rhombus.

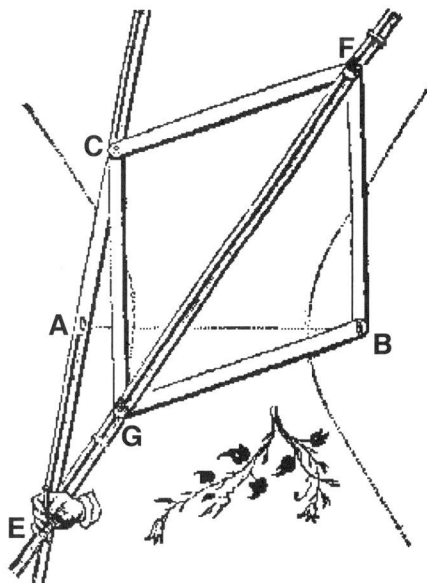

3. Open the sketch **van Schooten.gsp** in the **Hyperbola** folder. You'll see a working model of the linkage below from the seventeenth-century mathematician Frans van Schooten. Drag point C and observe the trace of point E.

   Can you prove that point E traces a hyperbola? The second page of the sketch contains some hints to get you started.

4. The sketch **Tangent Circles.gsp** in the **Hyperbola** folder shows a red circle c_3 that's simultaneously tangent to circles c_1 and c_2. Press the *Animate* button and observe the path of point C, the center of circle c_3. Can you prove that C traces a hyperbola?

5. Rectangular hyperbolas are of the form $xy = c$, where c is a constant. Open the multi-page sketch **Area.gsp** in the **Hyperbola** folder to learn about some applications of these curves.

4

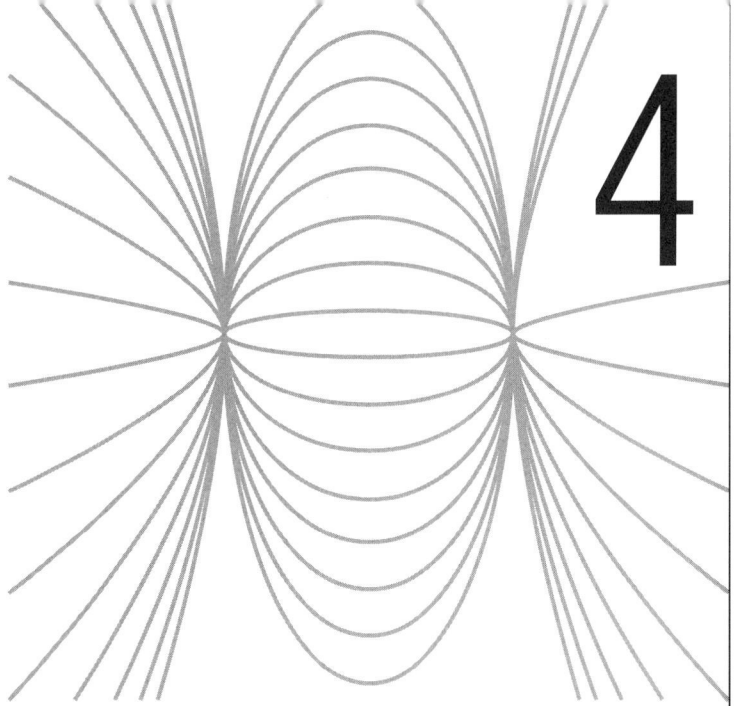

Optimization

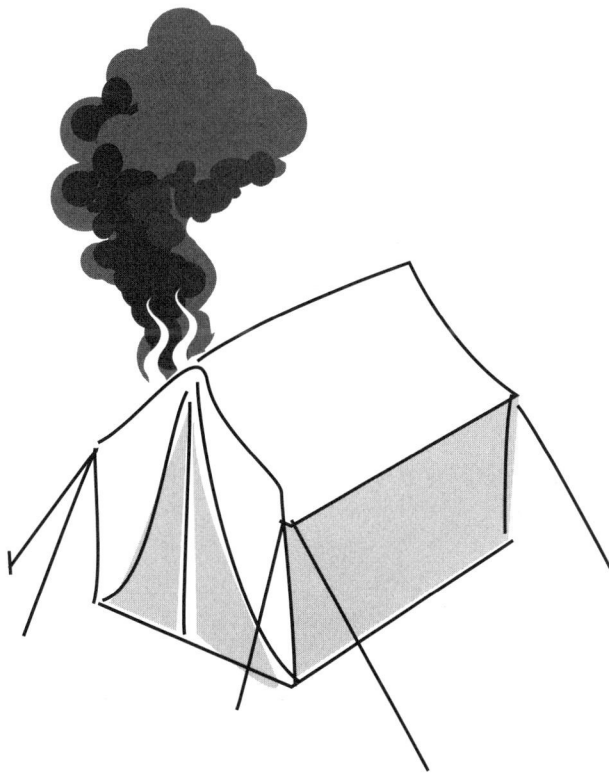

CHAPTER OVERVIEW

What do a burning tent, a circular swimming pool, and a cowgirl have in common? Nothing, perhaps, except that all three appear in this chapter in geometric optimization problems. Can you find a speedy path to your burning tent before only ashes remain? Can you swim to your friend with only a minimum of effort? Can you help a cowgirl lead her horse to food and water by plotting the shortest riding distance?

Normally, the topic of optimization doesn't arise until calculus, and there it is treated algebraically. Calculus is a great tool, but it's not the only way to solve optimization problems. There's only one prerequisite for this chapter—the Pins-and-String Construction from Chapter One. With that alone, you're ready to approach optimization problems from a purely geometric perspective. Follow the activities in the order listed—they're sequenced to build on each other.

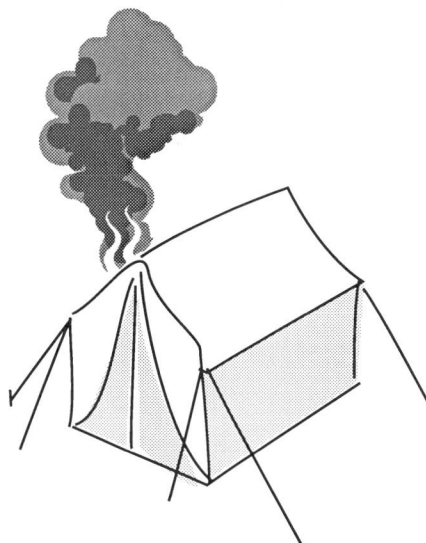

Ellipses aren't generally considered standard firefighting tools, but perhaps they should be . . .

I. The Burning Tent Problem

With your camping tent on fire, it's mathematics to the rescue as you determine the optimal location for collecting some much-needed water.

II. The Swimming Pool Problem

A lazy day in a swimming pool turns mathematical when you agree to buy the next round of ice teas for a friend. Can you find the shortest distance to paddle without breaking a sweat?

III. An Optimization Project

Apply your optimization knowledge to this cowgirl conundrum.

The Burning Tent Problem

Name(s): _____

Consider the following situation:

> Ah, the great outdoors. Camping, the fresh air, the starry night sky, and—fire! Your tent is ablaze! Fortunately, you (at point Y) have a bucket in hand. You decide to run to the river's edge, fill your bucket, and race to your tent (point T) to douse the flames.
>
> Where along the river should you head in order to minimize your total running distance? The picture below shows one possible location—point P—you might run to.

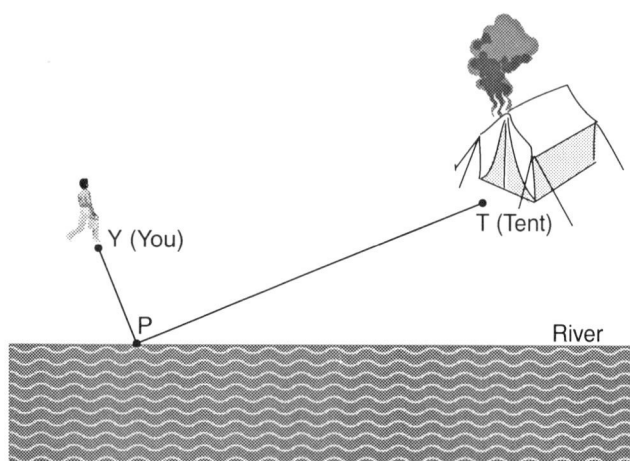

Yes, we admit it: If our tent were really on fire, we wouldn't stop to do math either!

This is an example of an *optimization* problem. You're trying to optimize the distance $YP + PT$ to make it as small as possible.

This problem can be solved algebraically, but it becomes very messy. So instead, you'll investigate the situation geometrically, first with string, then with Sketchpad.

Constructing a Physical Model

Preparation: You'll need a sheet of paper (larger is better), some string, a pencil, a ruler, and tape.

1. Draw a long line on your paper to represent the river's edge. Leave space below the line to represent the water. Draw two points, Y and T, to represent you and the tent.

2. Cut a length of string and attach its ends with tape or thumbtacks to points Y and T. If the string does not extend below the river's edge when pulled taut, cut a longer piece or relocate Y and T.

Questions

Q1 Without taking any measurements, use your string to find the optimal location along the river to run. Explain your method.

The Burning Tent Problem (continued)

The Burning Tent problem can be solved in several ways. The questions that follow describe one especially interesting technique. As you answer the questions, think about the similarities between your method for finding the optimal river location and the one presented here.

Before you begin, make sure your string is set up as before, with its ends attached to points Y and T. The string should be long enough to extend below the river's edge when pulled taut.

Q2 Use a pencil to pull the string taut so that the pencil point sits *directly* on the river's edge. Call this point P. Point P is one location along the river you might run to. It's probably not the best location, but it will serve as an initial guess.

Use your string to find another point along the river's edge equivalent to P in total running distance. Describe how you found the point.

Q3 Ignore, for a moment, the context of this problem. Use your string and a pencil to draw *all* points, whether on land or in the water, equivalent to P in total distance. Describe this set of points. What curve have you drawn?

Q4 Use the curve from Q3 to identify two intervals on the river's edge: those locations whose total running distance is less than that of P's and those locations whose total running distance is greater than that of P's.

Explain how you found these intervals.

Q5 How should you proceed in order to find the optimal location along the river?

Constructing a Sketchpad Model

The ideas behind the string solution to the Burning Tent problem can be applied to a corresponding Sketchpad model. Here's how:

3. Open the sketch **Burning Tent.gsp** in the **Optimization** folder. You'll see "you" (point Y), the tent (point T), and a point P along the river you might run to.

You may have built such a tool if you did Project 6 from Ellipse Projects (page 29). If so, use it instead.

4. Choose **Ellipse by Foci/Point** from the Custom Tools menu in the Toolbox. This tool takes any three points—F_1, F_2, and P—and constructs an ellipse with foci at F_1 and F_2, passing through point P.

Questions

Q6 Use the **Ellipse by Foci/Point** tool to find the optimal river location to run to. What is the relationship between the ellipse and the river at the optimal location?

Q7 Can there be more than one optimal location for a straight river? Explain.

Q8 Draw a curvy river (by hand, if you prefer) for which there are two optimal locations to run to. Include an ellipse in your drawing to justify your answer.

Q9 Suppose that regardless of where you ran to along the river's edge, the total distance from you (point Y) to the river to the tent (point T) was the same. What would such a river look like?

A Reflection Technique

The Burning Tent problem is quite old. It appears in the 1917 book *Amusements in Mathematics* by the great puzzlemaster Henry Ernest Dudeney, where it's called the "Milkmaid Puzzle."

Dudeney's method for solving the problem is totally different from the one you just used. Follow the steps below to understand his approach.

5. Open the sketch **Reflection.gsp** in the **Optimization** folder. You'll see you (point Y), the tent (point T), and an arbitrary point P along the river you might run to.

6. Double-click the line representing the river's edge to mark it as a mirror line of reflection. The line should flash briefly to indicate that it's been marked.

7. Select point T using the **Arrow** tool. Then choose **Reflect** from the Transform menu to reflect point T across the river's edge. Label the reflected point as T'.

8. Connect point P to point T' with a segment PT'.

Questions

Q10 Explain why the following equality holds for any location of point P:

$$YP + PT = YP + PT'$$

Q11 Based on the equality from Q10, explain how to find the optimal location of point P. Then use the ellipse tool to see if it yields the same result.

Q12 Solve this problem by reflecting point Y instead of point T.

The Swimming Pool Problem

Name(s): _____

Now that you've put out the flames from the Burning Tent, how about a well-earned rest? It's just you, a friend, and a swimming pool. But wouldn't you know it—the ellipse from the Tent problem returns! Read on . . .

Tea for Two

You (at point Y) and your friend (at point F) are floating on inflatable lounge chairs in a circular swimming pool. Waiters are positioned all around the edge of the pool, and it's your turn to buy two iced teas.

You'll need to paddle to the edge, buy the drinks, and deliver one to your friend. Where along the pool's edge should you paddle to in order to minimize the total distance? The picture below shows one possible path.

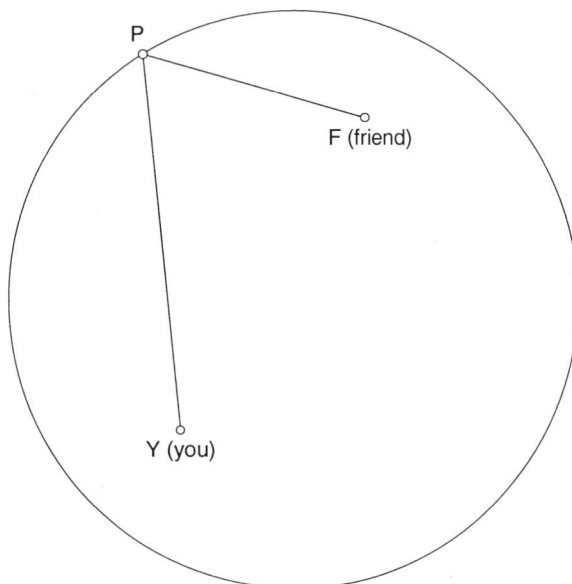

Try changing the location of points Y and F. Press the *Reset* button when you're done.

Open the first page of the sketch **Swimming Pool.gsp** in the **Optimization** folder. Besides the swimming pool, you'll see an ellipse with foci at points Y and F that passes through an arbitrary point P on the circle's circumference. Drag point P. The ellipse adjusts itself, with Y and F remaining the foci.

The Swimming Pool Problem (continued)

Questions

Q1 Notice that there are four positions of P where the ellipse is tangent to the circle. As with the Burning Tent, these locations are special. Use the four circles that follow to draw the four tangent ellipses.

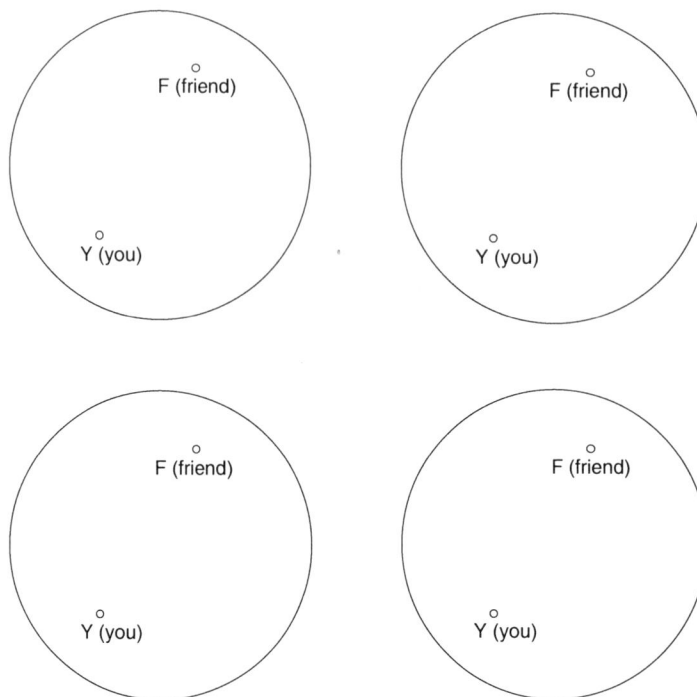

Q2 Now open the second page of the sketch and drag point P. You'll see that four locations on the circle's circumference—P_2 through P_5—correspond to the points of tangency you drew above. The sketch also includes two more points, P_1 and P_6, for reference.

Here, in no particular order, are descriptions of locations P_2 through P_5:

- This location gives the shortest overall paddling distance.
- This location gives the longest overall paddling distance.
- This location isn't the best, but it's better than all nearby locations on either side of it.
- This location isn't the worst, but it's worse than all nearby locations on either side of it.

Match the descriptions to the locations. Explain how the positions of the ellipse, relative to the pool, allowed you to draw your conclusions.

Q3 From shortest overall paddling distance to longest, rank the four locations P_2, P_3, P_4, and P_5.

Exploring Conic Sections with The Geometer's Sketchpad
© 2002 Key Curriculum Press

The Swimming Pool Problem (continued)

Q4 Below is a set of axes for graphing. The horizontal axis represents positions along the edge of the pool. For convenience, six locations are labeled—P_1 through P_6. (Imagine the pool's edge cut and then straightened into a segment.) The vertical axis represents the total distance it takes to paddle to your friend.

Use the information from Q2 and Q3 to draw a rough graph of the location along the edge versus total paddling distance. The graph need not represent the actual distances; rather, strive to make the *shape* of the graph and the *relative* heights at P_1 through P_6 as accurate as possible.

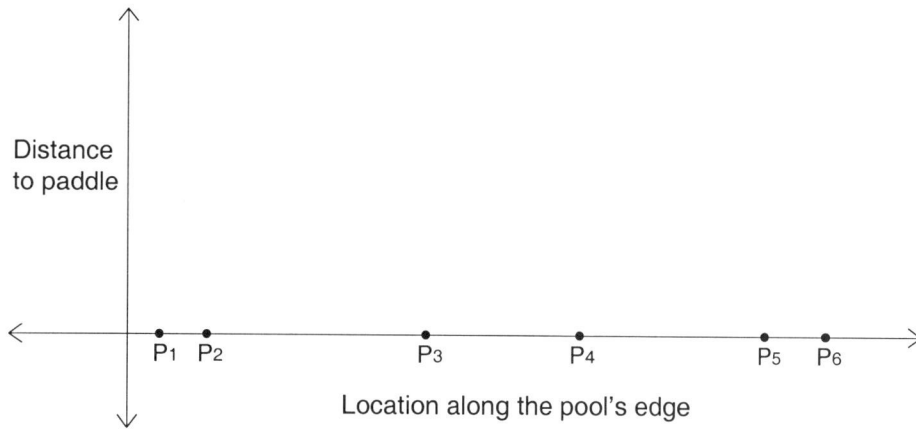

Distance to paddle

P_1 P_2 P_3 P_4 P_5 P_6

Location along the pool's edge

Q5 Believe it or not, you've just done some calculus! We use the following terms in calculus to describe points on a graph: *absolute maximum, absolute minimum, relative maximum, relative minimum.*

Make an educated guess as to the meanings of these terms, then match the terms to points P_2 through P_5.

Q6 If you open page 3 of **Swimming Pool.gsp** and press the *Show Graph* button, you'll see the graph from Q4. Experiment with its shape by moving the locations of Y and F.

How should Y and F be positioned to make the entire graph horizontal, or nearly so?

An Optimization Project

The project below builds on your knowledge from the Burning Tent and Swimming Pool problems.

The Cowgirl Problem

Open the sketch **Cowgirl.gsp** in the **Optimization** folder and consider the following situation:

> A cowgirl wants to give her horse some food and water before returning to her tent. She starts at point *C* and decides to travel first to the pasture, then to the river, and then back to her tent. What path should she take to minimize her riding distance?

Points *A* and *B* are two possible locations the cowgirl might take her horse to.

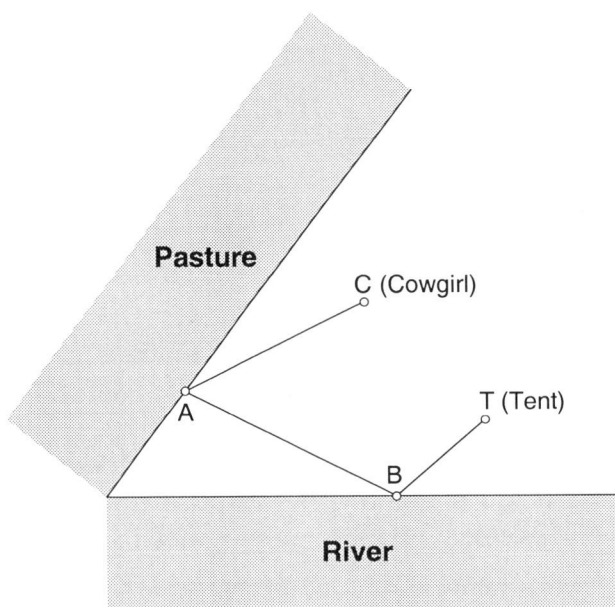

Solve this problem in two ways: with ellipses (use the provided custom tool) and by reflection. Does your solution change if the cowgirl decides to travel first to the river and then to the pasture?

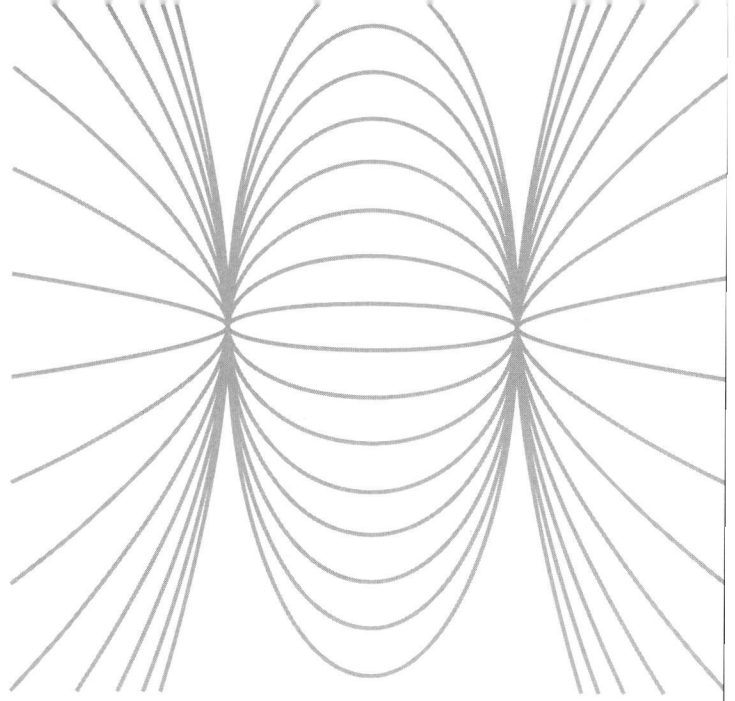

Activity Notes

Getting Started: When Is a Circle Not a Circle? (page 5)

Prerequisites: None.

Sketchpad Proficiency: Beginner.

Activity Time: 10 minutes.

General Notes: This activity provides a quick newcomer's introduction to ellipses and their focal points.

Follow-Up Activities: Continue with the Pins-and-String Construction.

The Pins-and-String Construction (page 6)

Prerequisites: The definition of "focal points" (discussed in the previous activity, Getting Started).

Sketchpad Proficiency: Beginner. Students use Sketchpad's measurement and calculation tools.

Activity Time: 40–50 minutes.

General Notes: This activity introduces the distance definition of an ellipse: The set of all points P such that $PF_1 + PF_2$ is constant for fixed points F_1 and F_2.

As an alternative to using a corkboard and thumbtacks, you can build your model by taping the ends of string onto a large piece of paper.

Students may need some help in moving from the pins-and-string model to the distance definition introduced in questions 9 and 10.

Follow-Up Activities: Both the Concentric Circles Construction and the Some Ellipse Relationships activities are good choices.

Constructing a Physical Model

Q1 The ellipse is symmetric across two lines. These lines (as defined in question 7) are perpendicular and called the *major* and *minor axes*.

The intersection of the two axes is the *center* of the ellipse. An ellipse has 180° rotational symmetry about its center.

Q2 When the ends of the string are farther apart, the ellipse is "skinnier" and more elongated.

Q3 When the ends of the string are close together, the ellipse is "fatter" and looks more like a circle.

Q4 The pencil will draw a line. This question and the next illustrate the two "degenerate" cases of an ellipse: a straight line and a circle.

Q5 When both ends of the string are attached to the same thumbtack, the pencil and string form a compass. Thus the pencil will draw a circle.

Q6 Your friend would need to know your length of string and the distance between the thumbtacks. (Of course, it would be difficult to reproduce the ellipse exactly without knowing how much of the string you used in tying knots around the thumbtacks!)

Q7 You might define the axes as the two perpendicular segments of symmetry, with the longer segment (the major axis) containing the focal points.

You might also define the axes as the longest and shortest segments that go through the "center" of the ellipse.

What happens when the ellipse is a circle? Do circles have major and minor axes?

Q8 Fold the paper ellipse twice so that its edges align perfectly each time. The longer crease is the major axis.

Uncover the Imposter

Q9 Draw segments from point A to F_1 and F_2. These represent a string attached to F_1 and F_2 pulled taut. Measured with Sketchpad, the total length of this "string" is 5.0 inches.

Now draw and measure the segments extending from point B to the foci and from point C to the foci. This reveals that $BF_1 + BF_2 = 5.0$ inches also, but $CF_1 + CF_2 = 5.3$ inches. Thus point C does not sit on the ellipse passing through points A and B.

Q10 An ellipse is the set of points P such that the following value is constant for all locations of P: $PF_1 + PF_2$, where F_1 and F_2 are the focal points.

The Concentric Circles Construction (page 8)

Prerequisites: The distance definition of an ellipse (discussed in the previous Pins-and-String Construction).

Sketchpad Proficiency: Intermediate. Students use Sketchpad's **Circle by Center+Radius** command and follow the steps of an extended construction. Alternatively, beginner students can view the pre-built sketch **Concentric Circles.gsp** (**Ellipse** folder).

Activity Time: 50–60 minutes. If time is short, use the pre-built sketch **Concentric Circles.gsp** (**Ellipse** folder).

General Notes: This activity provides a lot of practice in applying the distance definition of an ellipse. Students may need some help in understanding how the concentric circles can be used to measure distances.

Follow-Up Activities: Both the Some Ellipse Relationships and the Folded Circle Construction activities are good choices.

Sketching Ellipses by Hand

Q1 Point A sits on a circle with center at F_1 and radius of 3. Thus $AF_1 = 3$ units. Similarly, $AF_2 = 2$ units. Thus $AF_1 + AF_2 = 5$ units.

Q2 All points P that sit on the ellipse passing through point A must satisfy the equality $PF_1 + PF_2 = 5$ units. See the picture below.

Q3 All points P that sit on the ellipse passing through point B must satisfy the equality $PF_1 + PF_2 = 8$ units. See the picture below.

Q4

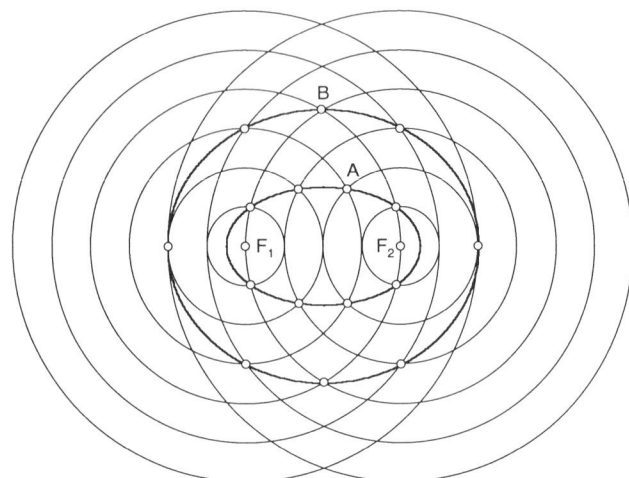

Constructing a Sketchpad Model

Q5 Regardless of point C's location, the sum of the two radii—$AC + CB$—is equal to the constant length AB.

Q6 Let P be an intersection point of the two circles. Then the distance from P to F_1 is AC, and the distance from P to F_2 is CB. Adding these two lengths together tells us that the combined distance of P from F_1 and F_2 is $AC + CB = AB$, which is constant. Thus the intersection points of the circles represent all points whose distances from F_1 and F_2 add up to the constant AB.

Q7 The distance between F_1 and F_2 must be less than the length of AB.

Q8 By dragging point C along $\overline{AB}$, you create two sets of concentric circles—one centered at F_1, the other centered at F_2. This Sketchpad model is a *continuous* version of what began as *discrete* concentric circles on paper.

Explore More

1. By adjusting the sketch's parameters, it's possible to draw a hyperbola. For more information, see the Concentric Circles Construction in the Hyperbola chapter.

2. The sketch **Constant Perimeter.gsp (Ellipse** folder) provides a model of such a rectangle.

Some Ellipse Relationships (page 11)

Prerequisites: The Pins-and-String Construction. Question 2 requires the Pythagorean theorem.

Sketchpad Proficiency: Beginner. Students manipulate a pre-built sketch and use Sketchpad's measurement and calculation tools.

Activity Time: 40–50 minutes.

General Notes: This activity introduces the algebraic relationships between an ellipse's major axis, minor axis, and focal points through an interactive geometric model.

Follow-Up Activities: The Folded Circle Construction.

Finding Lengths

Q1 Drag point P so that it lies atop point B. The "string" now lies flat along the major axis with a double thickness between points F_2 and B. (You might want to move point P slightly above point B to remind yourself of the two layers.)

Since $AF_1 = F_2B$, we can imagine moving one layer of the double thickness onto $\overline{AF_1}$. The major axis is thus equal in length to the string. $AB = 20$ cm.

Q2 Drag point P so that it lies atop point D. Triangle POF_2 is a right triangle, so by the Pythagorean theorem:

$$(OF_2)^2 + (OP)^2 = (PF_2)^2$$

Substituting $OF_2 = 8$ cm and $PF_2 = 10$ cm into the above equation and solving for OP yields $OP = 6$ cm. Thus the minor axis is 12 cm long.

Q3 Responses will vary.

Eccentricity

Q4 The eccentricity of an ellipse approaches 0 when the foci come close together. The eccentricity approaches 1 when the length of $\overline{F_1F_2}$ nears the length of $\overline{AB}$.

Eccentricities close to 0 produce an ellipse that is nearly a circle. Eccentricities *very* close to 1 produce an ellipse that is difficult to distinguish from a line segment.

Why do we emphasize the word *very*? Even an ellipse with an eccentricity of 0.99 is not nearly as flat as you might think. Try it with Sketchpad!

Q5 Since eccentricity is measured as a ratio, an infinite number of ellipses share the same eccentricity. Informally, equal-eccentricity ellipses have the same shape.

You can enlarge or reduce an ellipse with a photocopy machine to obtain another ellipse with the identical eccentricity.

Explore More

1. From question 2, we know that the distance from each focal point to point D is half the string's length.

   Thus, to find the ellipse's foci, build a circle centered at point D with radius equal to half the string length. The intersection points of this circle with the major axis determine the foci.

2. Pluto has the largest eccentricity with a value of 0.248. If you adjust the ellipse in **Eccentricity.gsp** to reflect this value, you'll see that the curve looks very circular.

The Folded Circle Construction (page 13)

Prerequisites: For students to complete the proof, they'll need to know the distance definition of an ellipse and the SAS triangle congruency theorem.

Sketchpad Proficiency: Intermediate. Students build a perpendicular bisector line and follow the steps of an extended construction. Alternatively, beginner students can view the sketch **Demo Model.gsp** (**Ellipse** folder), which contains pre-built models of everything.

Activity Time: 70–80 minutes. If time is short, use the pre-built sketch **Demo Model.gsp** (**Ellipse** folder). The proof can be assigned for homework.

General Notes: Of all the ellipse construction methods, this is the one most likely to elicit "oohs" and "aahs." Once students get the hang of folding their circles, they find it amazing to watch their creases gradually come together in the outline of an ellipse. The equivalent Sketchpad model is equally impressive.

Follow-Up Activities: The Folded Rectangle Construction (Parabola chapter) features the same paper-folding technique and proof method as this activity. Also see the second project listed in Ellipse Projects and the first project listed in Hyperbola Projects.

The Congruent Triangles Construction doesn't involve paper folding, but does share the same underlying geometry and proof structure as the Folded Circle.

Constructing a Physical Model

Q1 Points A and B are the foci.

Q2 The ellipse would appear "skinnier" and more elongated.

Q3 The ellipse would appear "fatter" and more like a circle.

Constructing a Sketchpad Model

In step 11, students must study the geometry of their crease lines. Specifically, given points C and B, how do you use Sketchpad to construct the "crease" formed when C is folded onto B? (The crease is the perpendicular bisector of segment CB.)

As preparation for this construction step, you might ask students to take a fresh sheet of notebook paper, mark two random points, fold one onto the other, then unfold the paper. What is the geometric relationship of the crease line to the two points?

Q4 The ellipse becomes "skinnier" and more elongated.

Q5 The ellipse becomes "fatter" and looks more like a circle.

Q6 The creases all pass through the circle's center, point A.

Q7 The creases outline a circle.

Playing Detective

In step 21, students are asked to construct the point of tangency to their ellipse. The point of tangency lies at the intersection of the crease line and segment AC.

How to Prove It

Q8 Since the crease line is the perpendicular bisector of segment BC, we have $DB = DC$ and $\angle EDB = \angle EDC = 90°$. And, of course, $ED = ED$. Thus, by the SAS triangle congruency theorem, $\triangle BED \cong \triangle CED$.

Q9 Since $\triangle BED \cong \triangle CED$, the corresponding sides BE and CE are equal.

Q10 If point E traces an ellipse, then $AE + BE$ must be constant. Substituting CE for BE gives:

$AE + BE = AE + CE = AC =$ the radius of the circle, which is constant

Explore More

1. When point B lies outside the circle, the creases outline a hyperbola. It's tempting to think that when point B lies *on* the circle, the creases will form a parabola, but, in fact, they don't! See the Folded Rectangle Construction for a paper-folded parabola.

2. $\angle AEH = \angle CED$, as they are vertical angles. Since $\triangle BED \cong \triangle CED$, we have $\angle CED = \angle BED$. Putting these two equalities together gives $\angle AEH = \angle BED$.

   (A full-page advertisement for elliptic pool tables appeared in the July 1, 1964, issue of *The New York Times*. Actors Paul Newman and Joanne Woodward made an in-store appearance to promote the game.

   On a related topic, students can search the Internet for information about the sound reflection properties of "whispering galleries.")

3. Points A and B are the foci of the ellipse.

   $BC + CA = (r + p) + (R - p) = r + R$, which is constant

The Congruent Triangles Construction (page 17)

Prerequisites: For students to complete the proof, they'll need to know the distance definition of an ellipse and the SSS and AAS triangle congruency theorems. If you omit the proof, there are no prerequisites.

Sketchpad Proficiency: Beginner.

Activity Time: 30–40 minutes. If time is short, you can assign the proof section for homework.

General Notes: Proving that this method yields ellipses provides a very nice application of triangle congruency.

Follow-Up Activity: The Folded Circle Construction shares the same underlying geometry and proof structure.

Questions

Q1 Points A and B are the foci.

Q2 The blue segment's length is equal to the distance between the foci. As it grows, the ellipse becomes more elongated.

Q3 The line represents the *tangent* to the ellipse at point E. In other words, it's the unique line passing through point E that touches the ellipse exactly once.

How to Prove It

Q4 We're given that $AB = FC$ and $BF = CA$. And, of course, $AF = AF$. Thus $\triangle ABF \cong \triangle FCA$ by the SSS triangle congruency theorem.

Q5 $\angle FCA = \angle ABF$

Q6 We know that $\angle FCA = \angle ABF$, $\angle FEC = \angle AEB$ (they're vertical angles) and $AB = FC$. Thus by the AAS triangle congruency theorem, $\triangle AEB \cong \triangle FEC$.

Intuitively, one can see that $\triangle AEB \cong \triangle FEC$ by noting that $\triangle AEB$ is the reflection of $\triangle FEC$ across the tangent line created in question 3.

Q7 Since $\triangle AEB \cong \triangle FEC$, their corresponding sides AE and FE are equal in length.

Q8 If point E traces an ellipse, then $AE + EB$ must be constant. Substituting FE for AE gives:

$AE + EB = FE + EB = BF =$ the length of the rod, which is constant

Explore More

1. Imagine twisting rod *FC* so that segments *BF* and *CA* no longer cross. The resulting quadrilateral, *ABFC*, is a parallelogram.

2. Point *C* traces a circle with center at point *A*. If you were to "fold" point *C* on the circle's circumference onto point *B*, the resulting crease would match the line you constructed in question 3.

4. For help in building the Congruent Triangles Construction from scratch, open the sketch **Congruent Triangles.gsp (Ellipse** folder) and choose **Show All Hidden** from the Display menu.

The Carpenter's Construction (page 19)

Prerequisites: For students to complete the proof, they'll need some familiarity with the Pythagorean theorem and either similar triangles or right-triangle trigonometry. The proof section provides a quick introduction to the algebraic form of ellipses, but you might want to consult a textbook first for more thorough coverage.

If you omit the proof, students will only need to know the definition of an ellipse's major and minor axes.

Sketchpad Proficiency: Beginner.

Activity Time: 70–80 minutes. If time is short, you can assign the proof section for homework.

General Notes: This activity features a device known as an *ellipsograph* or *trammel*. Compared to the standard pins-and-string technique offered in most textbooks (and here in the second activity), the ellipsograph offers the following advantages:

*   Drawing an ellipse with specified major and minor axes lengths is a straightforward process (see question 2).

*   Proving that the ellipsograph draws ellipses involves little algebraic messiness.

Follow-Up Activity: Danny's Ellipse shares a nearly identical proof structure, as does the Sliding Ladder in "Explore More" question 3.

Constructing a Physical Model

Q1 When point *B* is close to point *A*, the ruler draws a nearly circular ellipse. If you imagine standing at a distance from the ruler, it would be difficult to distinguish its movement from a compass.

When point *B* sits close to point *C*, the ellipse is "skinny" and elongated.

Q2 Length *AC* represents half the major axis of the ellipse and length *BC* represents half the minor axis. Thus you'd need to position the points so that $AB = 4$ cm and $BC = 6$ cm.

Q3 Strictly speaking, an ellipsograph cannot draw circles. Point *B* would need to sit atop point *A*.

How to Prove It

Q4 Given the lengths in the picture, we have an ellipse with major axis of length 18 and minor axis of length 6. Substituting $a = 3$ and $b = 9$ into the equation for an ellipse yields

$$\frac{x^2}{9} + \frac{y^2}{81} = 1$$

Q5 $BD = x$; $CE = y$; by the Pythagorean theorem, $CD = \sqrt{9 - x^2}$

Q6 First, let's solve this problem with similar triangles:

We have $\triangle ACE \sim \triangle BCD$, since both triangles contain right angles and AE is parallel to BD. Given this relationship, we can write the proportion

$$\frac{CE}{AC} = \frac{CD}{BC}$$

Substitute $AC = 9$, $BC = 3$, and the values from question 5 into this equation. Square both sides and rearrange the terms. You'll derive the predicted ellipse equation from question 4.

Now let's solve the problem using trigonometry:

Let $\angle CAE = \angle CBD = \theta$. Then from $\triangle ACE$ we have $\sin(\theta) = CE/AC$. And $\triangle BCD$ gives $\cos(\theta) = BD/BC$. Since $\sin^2(\theta) + \cos^2(\theta) = 1$, we can write

$$\left(\frac{y}{9}\right)^2 + \left(\frac{x}{3}\right)^2 = 1$$

Q7 The general equation is $\left(\dfrac{x}{t}\right)^2 + \left(\dfrac{y}{s+t}\right)^2 = 1$.

Explore More

1. For help in building an ellipsograph from scratch, open the first page of the sketch **Carpenter.gsp** (**Ellipse** folder) and choose **Show All Hidden** from the Display menu.

2. From the Some Ellipse Relationships activity (questions 1 and 2), we know that a segment extended from a focus to an endpoint of the minor axis is half the length of the major axis.

   Since $\overline{AC}$ is half the length of the major axis in the Carpenter's Construction, we build a circle with radius AC centered at endpoint D of the minor axis. The intersection points of this circle with the major axis determine the foci. See the third page of **Carpenter.gsp** for a picture.

3. The bucket traces a quarter ellipse (see the sketch **Ladder.gsp** in the **Ellipse** folder). To prove it does, draw segments through point E parallel to the x- and y-axes. Then, as with the ellipsograph, use either triangle similarity or trigonometry to derive the equation.

4. Call the ladder's endpoints A and B. The bucket sits midway between them at a point M. Let O be the point where the wall meets the ground.

   Since AOB is a right triangle, the theorem tells us that $OM = AM$. This relationship holds for any position of the ladder. Because length AM does not change, OM also remains constant. Thus, as the ladder slides down the wall, point M remains at a fixed distance from point O. Stated differently, point M traces a circle.

5. The second page of the sketch includes a short investigation and question.

Danny's Ellipse (page 25)

Prerequisites: For students to complete the proof, they'll need some familiarity with the Pythagorean theorem and either similar triangles or right-triangle trigonometry. The proof section provides a quick introduction to the algebraic form of ellipses, but you might want to consult a textbook first for more thorough coverage.

If you omit the proof, there are no prerequisites.

Sketchpad Proficiency: Intermediate. Students construct several perpendicular lines and follow the steps of an extended construction. Alternatively, beginner students can view the pre-built sketch **Danny.gsp** (**Ellipse** folder).

Activity Time: 60–70 minutes. If time is short, use the pre-built sketch, **Danny.gsp**. You might also assign the proof section for homework.

General Notes: Yes, Danny was a real student! In the early 1990s, Danny gave the folks at Key Curriculum Press a call and asked where he could find Sketchpad's "oval" tool. They told him that Sketchpad didn't come with a ready-made ellipse feature, but did suggest several ways to build the curve.

Danny wasn't too satisfied with what he heard. Surely, there had to be a simpler construction technique. Lo and behold, several months later Danny had devised his own method—the one presented in this activity.

Key Curriculum Press sponsored a contest with prizes for the five most original responses explaining whether Danny's "oval" was indeed an ellipse. Teachers and students from as far away as India wrote in to share their findings.

Follow-Up Activity: The Carpenter's Construction shares a nearly identical proof structure.

How to Prove It

Q1 Given the lengths in the picture, we have an ellipse with a major axis of length 10 and a minor axis of length 4. Substituting $a = 5$ and $b = 2$ into the equation for an ellipse yields

$$\frac{x^2}{25} + \frac{y^2}{4} = 1$$

Q2 $AG = x$; $EH = y$; by the Pythagorean theorem, $DG = \sqrt{25 - x^2}$.

Q3 First, let's solve this problem with similar triangles:

We have $\triangle AEH \sim \triangle ADG$, since both triangles contain right angles and EH is parallel to DG. Given this relationship, we can write the proportion

$$\frac{EH}{AE} = \frac{DG}{AD}$$

Substitute $AE = 2$, $AD = 5$, and the values from question 2 into this equation. Square both sides and rearrange the terms. You'll derive the predicted ellipse equation from question 1.

Now let's solve the problem using trigonometry:

Let $\angle A = \theta$. Then from $\triangle AEH$ we have $\sin(\theta) = EH / AE$. And $\triangle ADG$ gives $\cos(\theta) = AG / AD$. Since $\sin^2(\theta) + \cos^2(\theta) = 1$, we can write

$$\left(\frac{y}{2}\right)^2 + \left(\frac{x}{5}\right)^2 = 1$$

Q4 The general equation is $\left(\dfrac{x}{s+t}\right)^2 + \left(\dfrac{y}{s}\right)^2 = 1$.

Explore More

1. From the Some Ellipse Relationships activity (questions 1 and 2), we know that a segment extended from a focus to an endpoint of the minor axis is half the length of the major axis.

   Since AC is half the length of the major axis in Danny's ellipse, we build a circle with radius AC centered at endpoint B of the minor axis. The intersection points of this circle with the major axis determine the foci. See the third page of **Danny.gsp** for a picture.

Ellipse Projects (page 28)

1. The sketch **PA+2PB.gsp** (**Ellipse** folder) provides a model of the curve.

   For information on egg-shaped curves, see Chapters 3 and 4 of *The Last Recreations* by Martin Gardner (Springer-Verlag, 1997).

2. The diagonals of any rhombus are perpendicular bisectors of each other. In the given rhombus $FCGB$, the rod through F and G is the perpendicular bisector of segment BC. Thus, when viewed in relation to the Folded Circle, line FG represents the crease line formed when point C is folded onto point B. (Note that point C traces a circle when dragged.)

5. The proof here follows the suggestions on page 3 of the sketch **Bent Straw.gsp** (**Ellipse** folder):

   $AF = x$; $DF = y$; $DC = 2$; $FC = \sqrt{4 - y^2}$; $BE = 3$
   ($\triangle BED$ is isosceles)

   We have $\triangle CDF \sim \triangle AEF$, since both triangles contain right angles and $\angle A = \angle C$. ($\triangle BAC$ is isosceles.) Given this relationship, we can write the proportion

   $$\frac{CF}{CD} = \frac{AF}{AE}$$

   Substituting values into this equation, squaring both sides, and rearranging the terms yields

   $$\frac{x^2}{64} + \frac{y^2}{4} = 1$$

Introducing the Parabola (page 34)

Prerequisites: None, though you may need to discuss how to measure the distance from a point to a line.

Sketchpad Proficiency: Beginner. Students construct a single perpendicular line.

Activity Time: 60–70 minutes.

General Notes: This activity introduces the distance definition of parabolas as well as the terms *focus* and *directrix*.

Follow-Up Activity: The Folded Rectangle Construction uses the distance definition of a parabola introduced here.

Defining a Parabola

Q1 Construct a segment from P to d that's perpendicular to line d. The length of the segment represents the distance from P to d.

Q2 The lengths of the segments should be equal to the distances already measured on screen.

Q3 Construct a segment through the focus perpendicular to the directrix. The midpoint of this segment is the parabola's vertex.

The Concentric Circles Method

Q4 Points A and B are 4 units apart, as are point B and line 1. Thus point B sits on a parabola with point A as its focus and line 1 as its directrix.

Q5–7

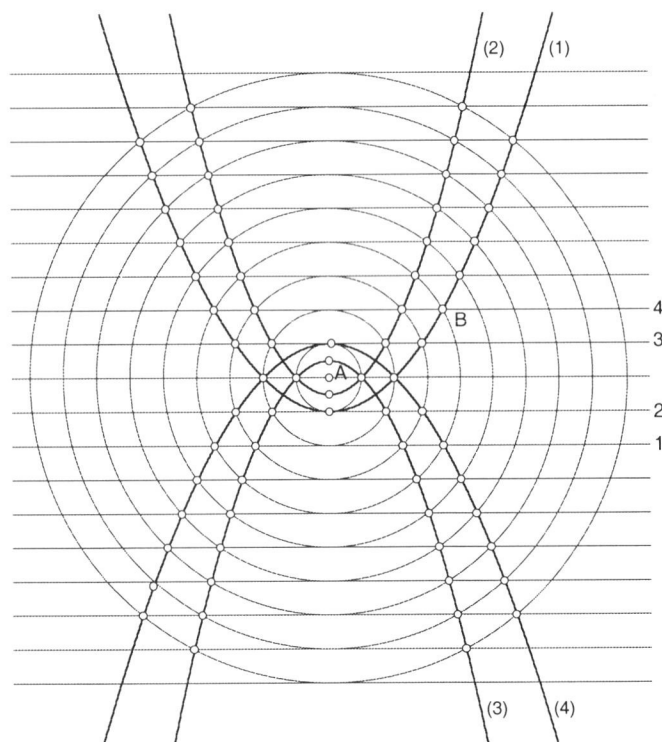

The Sliding Ruler Method

Q8 Point A is the focus and the upper edge of the horizontal ruler is the directrix.

Q9 You must prove that $CA = CD$.

Q10 Since the string ($BC + CA$) is equal in length to the ruler BD, we have $BC + CA = BC + CD$.

Q11 Subtracting BC from both sides of the equality in question 10 yields $CA = CD$.

The Folded Rectangle Construction (page 38)

Prerequisites: For students to complete the proof, they'll need to know the distance definition of a parabola and the SAS triangle congruency theorem.

Sketchpad Proficiency: Intermediate. Students build a perpendicular bisector line and follow the steps of an extended construction. Alternatively, beginner students can view the sketch **Demo Model.gsp (Parabola** folder), which contains pre-built models of everything.

Activity Time: 70–80 minutes. If time is short, use the pre-built sketch **Demo Model.gsp (Parabola** folder). The activity will likely take less time if you've done the Folded Circle Construction from the Ellipse chapter.

General Notes: The paper-folding technique in this activity is a simple and impressive way to generate parabolas. In fact, since all it requires is a single sheet of paper, this method can be downright addictive. Got a blank sheet of paper? Fold a parabola!

Follow-Up Activities: The Folded Circle Construction (Ellipse chapter) features the same paper-folding technique and could be assigned as an independent project.

Also see the third project listed in Parabola Projects.

Constructing a Physical Model

Q1 Point A is the focus and the bottom edge of the paper is the directrix.

Q2 The curve would appear "narrower."

Constructing a Sketchpad Model

In step 10, students must study the geometry of their crease lines. Specifically, given points B and A, how do you use Sketchpad to construct the "crease" formed when B is folded onto A? (The crease is the perpendicular bisector of segment AB.)

As preparation for this construction step, you might ask students to take a fresh sheet of notebook paper, mark two random points, fold one onto the other, then unfold the paper. What is the geometric relationship of the crease line to the two points?

Q3 As point A approaches the horizontal line, the curve appears "narrower."

Q4 As point A moves away from the horizontal line, the curve appears "wider."

Playing Detective

In step 19, students are asked to construct the point of tangency to their parabola. To do so, construct a line k through point B perpendicular to the horizontal line. The point of tangency lies at the intersection of line k with the crease line.

It's interesting to consider whether a parabola has asymptotes; that is, if there are lines the curve approaches but never crosses. By observing the tangent line as point B moves farther and farther away from the focus, we see that the curve becomes more and more perpendicular to the directrix. So if there are asymptotes, they must be perpendicular to the directrix.

But given any perpendicular, there is a point on it that is equidistant from the focus and the directrix. Thus the curve crosses the line, and the line cannot be an asymptote.

How to Prove It

Q5 You must prove that $AD = DB$.

Q6 Since the crease line is the perpendicular bisector of segment AB, we have $CA = CB$ and $\angle ACD = \angle BCD = 90°$. And, of course, $CD = CD$. Thus, by the SAS triangle congruency theorem, $\triangle ACD \cong \triangle BCD$.

Q7 Since $\triangle ACD \cong \triangle BCD$, corresponding sides AD and DB are equal in length.

Explore More

1. Since the circle is tangent to the line at point B, the radius CB is perpendicular to the line. Thus segment CB represents the distance of point C from the line. Segments CB and CA are both radii of the circle and equal in length. Therefore C traces a parabola with a focus at point A.

2. As point A travels farther and farther off screen, the portion of the circle we see gets straighter and straighter. When point A finally stops moving, we're left with a construction that looks like the Folded Rectangle—a single focus (point B) and a nearly flat directrix.

3. $\angle GDF = \angle BDC$, as they are vertical angles. Since $\triangle ADC \cong \triangle BDC$, we have $\angle ADC = \angle BDC$. Putting these two equalities together gives $\angle GDF = \angle ADC$.

The Expanding Circle Construction (page 42)

Prerequisites: For students to complete the proof, they'll need some information about geometric means (provided in the activity) and the algebraic definition of a parabola. If you omit the proof, there are no prerequisites.

Sketchpad Proficiency: Intermediate. Students construct several perpendicular lines and follow the steps of an extended construction. Alternatively, beginner students can view the pre-built sketch **Expanding Circle.gsp** (**Parabola** folder).

Activity Time: 60–70 minutes. If time is short, use the pre-built sketch **Expanding Circle.gsp** (**Parabola** folder).

General Notes: This activity provides a contrast to the Folded Rectangle Construction as it highlights the algebraic, as opposed to distance definition, of a parabola.

Constructing a Sketchpad Model

Q1 The curve always passes through point A and is symmetric across the y-axis, but it appears to become wider as point B is dragged downward.

Q2 If you had only a compass and straightedge available, you would need to draw a collection of individual circles, each passing through point B with a center somewhere along the positive y-axis. Then, moving from circle to circle, you would construct the necessary lines to locate points G and H (a pair of points for each circle). Using graph paper could help by providing rough guidelines for the perpendiculars.

The Geometric Mean

Q3 The proof below follows the setup on the second page of the sketch **Geometric Mean.gsp** (**Parabola** folder).

As all angles inscribed in a semicircle are right angles, $\angle DGE = 90°$. Since $\angle GDF + \angle DGF = 90° = \angle EGF + \angle DGF$, we have $\angle GDF = \angle EGF$. Thus right triangles DFG and GFE are similar. Based on this similarity, we can write the proportion

$$\frac{DF}{GF} = \frac{FG}{FE} \text{ or equivalently, } \frac{a}{x} = \frac{x}{b}.$$

Cross-multiplying gives $x^2 = ab$.

How to Prove It

Q4 $AF = x$; $AD = y$

Q5 $(AF)^2 = (AB)(AD)$ or equivalently, $x^2 = 3y$

Q6 Point G is the reflection of point H across the y-axis. Since the y-axis serves as the parabola's line of symmetry, point G must also sit on the parabola.

Q7 When $AB = s$, we have $x^2 = sy$.

Explore More

1. Return to your expanding circle sketch and add segments DE and EB to the construction. As you drag point C, notice that $\triangle DEB$ remains a right triangle as it is inscribed in a semicircle.

Parabola Projects (page 45)

2. Use the technique from the Folded Rectangle activity to build a parabola, its focus, and its directrix. Then select these elements to build a custom tool.

3. The diagonals of any rhombus are perpendicular bisectors of each other. In the given rhombus *EBFA,* the rod through *E* and *F* is the perpendicular bisector of segment *AB.* Thus when viewed in relation to the Folded Rectangle, line *ED* represents the crease line formed when point *B* is folded onto point *A.* The track along which point *B* moves represents the edge of the rectangle.

Introducing the Hyperbola (page 50)

Prerequisites: None.

Sketchpad Proficiency: Beginner.

Activity Time: 30–40 minutes.

General Notes: This activity introduces the distance definition of the hyperbola through an engaging buried treasure application.

'X' Marks the Spot

Drag the uppermost segment in the sketch to make the constant difference in hyperbola 1 equal to two. Since the treasure is two miles farther from point B than from point L, it sits somewhere along the right branch of hyperbola 1.

Now drag the lower segment in the sketch to make the constant difference in hyperbola 2 equal to three. Since the treasure is three miles farther from point C than from point J, it sits somewhere along the upper branch of hyperbola 2.

Thus, the treasure sits at the intersection of the two hyperbola branches described above.

(The buried treasure context of this problem is fanciful, but the method itself is used by hyperbolic navigation systems such as Loran. Two pairs of stations (A, B and C, D) send out radio signals simultaneously. A ship or plane notes the time difference in receiving the signals from A and B, as well as from C and D. These differences determine two hyperbolas whose intersection marks the location of the ship or plane.)

The Concentric Circles Construction (page 52)

Prerequisites: The previous activity, Introducing the Hyperbola.

Sketchpad Proficiency: Beginner.

Activity Time: 50–60 minutes.

General Notes: This activity offers two construction methods based on the distance definition of the hyperbola.

Q1 Point A sits on a circle with center at F_1 and radius of 4. Thus, $AF_1 = 4$ units. Similarly, $AF_2 = 3$ units. Thus, $AF_1 - AF_2 = 1$ unit.

Q2 All points P that sit on the hyperbola passing through point A must satisfy the equality $|PF_1 - PF_2| = 1$ unit. See the picture below.

Q3 All points P that sit on the hyperbola passing through point B must satisfy the equality $|PF_1 - PF_2| = 2$ units. See the picture below.

Q4

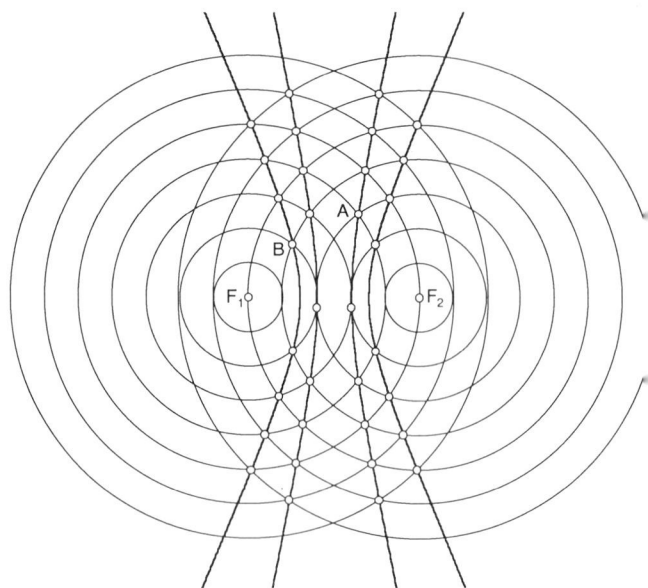

Q5 Regardless of point C's location to the right or left of $\overline{AB}$, the difference of the two radii, AC and BC, is equal to the constant length AB.

Q6 Let P be an intersection point of the two circles. Then the distance from P to F_1 is AC, and the distance from P to F_2 is BC. Subtracting these two values gives the constant length AB. Thus, P traces a hyperbola with a constant difference of AB.

Q7 By dragging point C, you create two sets of concentric circles—one centered at F_1, the other centered at F_2. This Sketchpad model is a *continuous* version of what began as *discrete* concentric circles on paper.

Q8 You must prove that $\left| AF_2 - AF_1 \right|$ is constant.

Q9 $BA + AF_2$ is the total length of the ruler, which is constant. $BA + AF_1$ is the length of the string, which is also constant. Thus the difference of these constant values is itself constant.

Q10 Simplifying the expression in question 9 (eliminating the two BA's) yields the desired result.

Hyperbola Projects (page 55)

1. Open page two of the sketch **Folded Circle Revisited.gsp**. To prove that the locus of creases traces a hyperbola, we must determine which point on the crease line is tangent to the curve.

   In the case of the ellipse, the tangency point sat at the intersection of the crease with segment AC. Here, the tangency point (point E) sits at the intersection of the crease with the *line* through point AC.

   As with the Folded Circle ellipse, $\triangle BED \cong \triangle CED$, making $EB = EC$. If point E traces a hyperbola with foci at points A and B, then $EB - EA$ must be constant. We have:

   $EB - EA = EC - EA = AC =$ the radius of the circle, which is constant

2. The diagonals of any rhombus are perpendicular bisectors of each other. In the given rhombus $FBGC$, the rod through F and G is the perpendicular bisector of segment BC. Thus, when viewed in relation to Project 1, line FE represents the crease line formed when point B is folded onto point C. (Note that point C traces a circle when dragged.)

3. We're given that $CF = BA$ and $AC = FB$. Combining these equalities with $AF = AF$ gives $\triangle ACF \cong \triangle FBA$ by the SSS triangle congruency theorem.

   Since $\triangle ACF \cong \triangle FBA$, we have $\angle ACF = \angle FBA$. So by the AAS triangle congruency theorem, $\triangle ECF \cong \triangle EBA$. Thus corresponding triangle sides EF and EA are equal.

   $EB - EA = EB - EF = FB$, which is constant. This tells us that point E traces a hyperbola with foci at points A and B.

4. The labeling below refers to the setup on page two of **Tangent Circles.gsp**:

   $AC - BC = (R + p) - (r + p) = R - r$, which is constant. Thus, point C traces a hyperbola with foci at points A and B.

The Burning Tent Problem (page 60)

Prerequisites: Familiarity with the Pins-and-String Construction activity in the Ellipse chapter.

Sketchpad Proficiency: Beginner. Students use a pre-built custom ellipse tool.

Activity Time: 70–80 minutes.

General Notes: The Burning Tent Problem is a staple of puzzle books and texts. Almost always, it's solved by performing a reflection. That method is clever, but often leaves students wondering, "How in the world did someone think of that?"

In this activity, students do examine the reflection technique, but first they solve the Burning Tent Problem on their own by using just a piece of string. Not only does this allow them to approach the problem in a more natural way, but it also leads nicely into a solution technique involving ellipses.

As you'll see, the ellipse method is really something: It's elegant, visual, and perfectly suited for the dynamic manipulation abilities of Sketchpad.

Follow-Up Activity: The Swimming Pool Problem.

Constructing a Physical Model

Q1 This question invites multiple solution methods and was written in a deliberately open-ended fashion. Before offering students assistance, see what ideas they suggest. Here are several approaches, all of which work well:

- Pick any point P along the river, pull the string taut at P, and pinch the excess string into a loop dangling below P. Extend the hanging loop straight down with your other hand to judge how much string sits below the river's edge. Adjust the location and amount of your pinch to maximize (by eye) the length of the loop. The location along the river where the pinch produces the longest loop represents the optimal running spot.

- Unfasten one end of the string and snip off a tiny piece. Reattach the string. Pull the string taut. If the string can be extended below the river's edge, cut it some more. Repeat this process with the string until it reaches exactly to the river's edge but not below.

- It's possible that students might solve this problem by using an ellipse. Wonderful! See questions 2 through 5.

Having found the best river location, students often suggest two plausible hypotheses:

- The angle formed by the taut string at the optimal river location is 90°.

- A line through the midpoint of segment YT perpendicular to the river's edge intersects the river at the optimal location.

Neither observation is, in fact, true. Students can check these conjectures with Sketchpad by drawing the Burning Tent setup, measuring the lengths of YP and PT with the software, and calculating their sum. As students drag point P along the river, they can determine which location yields the shortest distance. (It will help to first increase the precision of the distance measurements in the Preferences panel.)

Q2 Keeping the string taut, pull the pencil point until it once again sits directly on the river's edge. This new location—call it point Q—is equivalent to point P in total running distance.

Q3 Pull the string taut with your pencil and then trace the path of the pencil point. From the Pins-and-String Construction, we know that the resulting curve is an ellipse. The ellipse intersects the river twice: once at point P, once at point Q.

Q4 All those points along the river's edge sitting inside the ellipse (between P and Q) represent shorter running distances. All other river points sitting outside the ellipse represent longer running distances.

Q5 Shorten the string (or pinch it) and draw a new ellipse that's smaller than the original. Let's assume that this new ellipse continues to intersect the river's edge twice, now at points P' and Q'. Somewhere between points P' and Q' lies the optimal river location. Since segment $P'Q'$ is shorter than PQ, we've narrowed the possibilities. Continue shortening the length of string and drawing new ellipses until an ellipse touches the river's edge exactly once. This point of tangency represents the optimal river location.

Mull this over for a while. It's pretty amazing!

Constructing a Sketchpad Model

Q6 Use the custom tool to construct an ellipse with foci at points Y and T passing through point P. Drag point P until the ellipse is tangent to the river. (The exact point of tangency can be a little hard to judge.) This point of tangency represents the optimal river location.

The sketch **Burning Tent Demo.gsp** (**Optimization** folder) contains a pre-built model with the ellipse already constructed.

Q7 Suppose the ellipse is tangent to the river at point R. Then every other point along the river's edge represents a greater running distance. Thus none of these points can be as good as point R.

Q8 The picture below shows a curvy river that's simultaneously tangent to an ellipse at points R and S. Both locations are optimal.

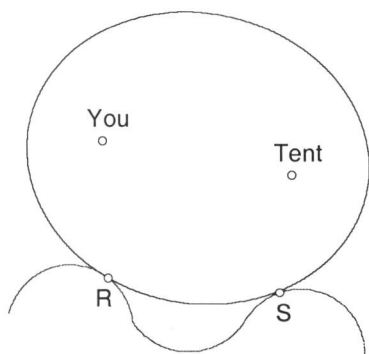

Q9 The river's edge would coincide exactly with an ellipse whose focal points sat at Y and T. You might also imagine that you're stranded on an elliptic island, surrounded on all sides by water. You're standing on one focal point of the island and your tent is at the other. No matter where along the island's shore you run, the distance $YP + PT$ will be the same.

A Reflection Technique

For those who might be interested, here is the context of Dudeney's "Milkmaid Puzzle":

"In the corner of a field is seen a milkmaid milking a cow, and on the other side of the field is the dairy where the extract has to be deposited. But it has been noticed that the young woman always goes down to the river with her pail before returning to the dairy. Here the suspicious reader will perhaps ask why she pays these visits to the river. I can only reply that it is no business of ours. The alleged milk is entirely for local consumption."

The third page of the sketch **Burning Tent Demo.gsp** (**Optimization** folder) contains a pre-built model of the reflection technique.

Q10 Let point D be the intersection of segment TT' with the river. By the properties of reflection, $DT = DT'$ and TT' is perpendicular to the river. Thus $\triangle PDT \cong \triangle PDT'$ by SAS and $PT = PT'$.

Q11 From question 10, we know that traveling from point Y to P to T is equivalent to traveling from point Y to P to T'. Thus minimizing $YP + PT$ is the same as minimizing $YP + PT'$. So what location of point P along the river's edge gives the smallest value of $YP + PT$?

The shortest distance between points Y and T' is a straight path. Connect points Y and T' with a segment. The intersection of $\overline{YT'}$ with the river's edge gives the optimal location of point P.

Q12 Reflect point Y to obtain Y'. Connect Y' to T. The intersection of $\overline{Y'T}$ with the river's edge gives the same optimal location as derived in question 11.

The Swimming Pool Problem (page 63)

Prerequisites: The Burning Tent Problem.

Sketchpad Proficiency: Beginner.

Activity Time: 50–60 minutes.

General Notes: This activity builds upon students' ellipse work from the Burning Tent Problem. Students draw a graph and identify its absolute maximum and minimum, as well as relative max's and min's, *all without a single bit of algebra or derivatives!* Geometry rules the day here.

Current research tells us that students' introduction to the underlying concepts of calculus should begin well before their first calculus course. When carefully studied, the Swimming Pool Problem is approachable by a wide range of students.

Follow-Up Activity: The Cowgirl Problem.

Tea for Two

Q1 The second page of the sketch **Swimming Pool.gsp** (**Optimization** folder) shows the four tangent positions P_2 through P_5.

Q2 P_5 gives the shortest overall paddling distance.

P_2 gives the longest overall paddling distance.

P_3 isn't the best location, but it's better than all nearby spots.

P_4 isn't the worst location, but it's worse than all nearby spots.

****

When the ellipse is tangent to the pool at point P_5, all other points along the pool lie outside the ellipse. Thus, P_5 gives the shortest overall paddling distance.

When the ellipse is tangent to the pool at point P_2, all other points along the pool sit inside the ellipse. Thus, P_2 gives the longest overall paddling distance.

When the ellipse is tangent to the pool at point P_3, all nearby points along the pool lie outside the ellipse. So P_3 is a good place to paddle in comparison to its neighbors. But farther away, there's an interval of the pool that sits inside the ellipse. Points along this interval represent shorter paddling distances. Thus, P_3 isn't the best location, but it's better than all nearby spots.

When the ellipse is tangent to the pool at point P_4, all nearby points along the pool sit inside the ellipse. So P_4 isn't a great place to paddle in comparison to its neighbors. But farther away, there's an interval of the pool that sits outside the ellipse. Points along this interval represent longer paddling distances. Thus, P_4 isn't the worst location, but it's worse than all nearby spots.

Q3 From shortest to longest paddling distances, we have: P_5, P_3, P_4, P_2.

Q4 To see the graph, open the third page of **Swimming Pool.gsp** and click on Show Graph. Your graph probably won't look identical, because you didn't know the actual paddling distances. What's important is the shape of your graph—does it display the correct relative heights and turning points?

Q5 Absolute maximum = P_2

Absolute minimum = P_5

Relative maximum = P_4

Relative minimum = P_3

Q6 Moving points Y and F directly onto the circle's center creates a horizontal graph. (In this instance the paddling distance is always $2r$, where r is the radius of the swimming pool.)

It's also possible to position points Y and F at distinct locations away from the center so that the ellipse nearly coincides with the circle. In these cases, the graph is fairly flat.

An Optimization Project (page 66)

Prerequisites: The Burning Tent activity.

Sketchpad Proficiency: Beginner. Students use a pre-built custom ellipse tool.

General Notes: For students who would like help in understanding the ellipse and reflection methods, the multi-page sketch **Demo Models.gsp** (**Optimization** folder) provides pre-built models and explanations.

Steven Harris, a student of mine at New York University, was, to my knowledge, the first to suggest the double-ellipse solution to this problem.